Theories of Psychotherapy Series
Jon Carlson and Matt Englar-Carlson, Series Editors

Person-Centered Psychotherapies

David J. Cain

American Psychological Association

Washington, DC

Published by
American Psychological Association
750 First Street, NE
Washington, DC 20002
www.apa.org

To order
APA Order Department
P.O. Box 92984
Washington, DC 20090-2984
Tel: (800) 374-2721;
Direct: (202) 336-5510
Fax: (202) 336-5502;
TDD/TTY: (202) 336-6123
Online: www.apa.org/books/
E-mail: order@apa.org

In the U.K., Europe, Africa, and the Middle East, copies may be ordered from
American Psychological Association
3 Henrietta Street
Covent Garden, London
WC2E 8LU England

Typeset in Minion by Shepherd Inc., Dubuque, IA

Printer: United Book Press, Inc., Baltimore, MD
Cover Designer: Minker Design, Sarasota, FL
Cover Art: Lily Rising, 2005, oil and mixed media on panel in craquelure frame, by Betsy Bauer.

The opinions and statements published are the responsibility of the authors, and such opinions and statements do not necessarily represent the policies of the American Psychological Association.

Library of Congress Cataloging-in-Publication Data

Cain, David J.
 Person-centered psychotherapies / David J. Cain. — 1st ed.
   p. ; cm. — (APA theories of psychotherapy series)
 Includes bibliographical references and index.
 ISBN-13: 978-1-4338-0721-3
 ISBN-10: 1-4338-0721-1
 1. Client-centered psychotherapy. I. American Psychological Association. II. Title. III. Series: APA theories of psychotherapy series.
 [DNLM: 1. Nondirective Therapy—methods. 2. Psychological Theory. WM 420.5.N8 C135p 2010]
 RC481.C28 2010
 616.89'14—dc22
                              2009041275

British Library Cataloguing-in-Publication Data
A CIP record is available from the British Library.

Printed in the United States of America
First Edition

Contents

Series Preface

Some might argue that in the contemporary clinical practice of psychotherapy, evidence-based intervention and effective outcome have overshadowed theory in importance. Maybe. But, as the editors of this series, we don't propose to take up that controversy here. We do know that psychotherapists adopt and practice according to one theory or another because their experience, and decades of good evidence, suggests that having a sound theory of psychotherapy leads to greater therapeutic success. Still, the role of theory in the helping process can be hard to explain. This narrative about solving problems helps convey theory's importance:

> Aesop tells the fable of the sun and wind having a contest to decide who was the most powerful. From above the earth, they spotted a man walking down the street, and the wind said that he bet he could get his coat off. The sun agreed to the contest. The wind blew and the man held on tightly to his coat. The more the wind blew, the tighter he held. The sun said it was his turn. He put all of his energy into creating warm sunshine and soon the man took off his coat.

What does a competition between the sun and the wind to remove a man's coat have to do with theories of psychotherapy? We think this deceptively simple story highlights the importance of theory as the precursor to any effective intervention—and hence to a favorable outcome. Without a guiding theory, we might treat the symptom without understanding the role of the individual. Or we might create power conflicts with our clients and not understand that, at times, indirect means of helping (sunshine) are often as effective—if not more so—than direct ones (wind). In the absence of theory, we might lose track of the treatment rationale and instead get caught up in, for example, social correctness and not wanting to do something that looks too simple.

What exactly *is* theory? The *APA Dictionary of Psychology* defines theory as "a principle or body of interrelated principles that purports to explain or predict a number of interrelated phenomena." In psychotherapy, a theory is a set of principles used to explain human thought and behavior, including what causes people to change. In practice, a theory creates the goals of therapy and specifies how to pursue them. Haley (1997) noted that a theory of psychotherapy ought to be simple enough for the average therapist to understand, but comprehensive enough to account for a wide range of eventualities. Furthermore, a theory guides action toward successful outcomes while generating hope in both the therapist and client that recovery is possible.

Theory is the compass that allows psychotherapists to navigate the vast territory of clinical practice. In the same ways that navigational tools have been modified to adapt to advances in thinking and ever-expanding territories to explore, theories of psychotherapy have changed over time. The different schools of theories are commonly referred to as waves, the first wave being psychodynamic theories (i.e., Adlerian, psychoanalytic), the second wave learning theories (i.e., behavioral, cognitive–behavioral), the third wave humanistic theories (person-centered, gestalt, existential), the fourth wave feminist and multicultural theories, and the fifth wave postmodern and constructivist theories. In many ways, these waves represent how psychotherapy has adapted and responded to changes in psychology, society, and epistemology as well as to changes in the nature of psychotherapy itself. Psychotherapy and the theories that guide it are dynamic and responsive. The wide variety of theories is also testament to the different ways in which the same human behavior can be conceptualized (Frew & Spiegler, 2008).

It is with these two concepts in mind—the central importance of theory and the natural evolution of theoretical thinking—that we developed the APA Theories of Psychotherapy Series. Both of us are thoroughly fascinated by theory and the range of complex ideas that drive each model. As university faculty members who teach courses on the theories of psychotherapy, we wanted to create learning materials that not only highlight the essence of the major theories for professionals and professionals in training but also clearly bring the reader up to date on the current status of the models. Often in books on theory, the biography of the original theorist overshadows the evolution of the model. In contrast, our intent is to highlight the contemporary uses of the theories as well as their history and context.

As this project began, we faced two immediate decisions: which theories to address and who best to present them. We looked at graduate-level theories of psychotherapy courses to see which theories are being taught, and we explored popular scholarly books, articles, and conferences to determine which theories draw the most interest. We then developed a dream list of authors from among the best minds in contemporary theoretical practice. Each author is one of the leading proponents of that approach as well as a knowledgeable practitioner. We asked each author to review the core constructs of the theory, bring the theory into the modern sphere of clinical practice by looking at it through a context of evidence-based practice, and clearly illustrate how the theory looks in action.

There are 24 titles planned for the series. Each title can stand alone or can be put together with a few other titles to create materials for a course in psychotherapy theories. This option allows instructors to create a course featuring the approaches they believe are the most salient today. To support this end, APA Books has also developed a DVD for each of the approaches that demonstrates the theory in practice with a real client. Many of the DVDs show therapy over six sessions. Contact APA Books for a complete list of available DVD programs (http://www.apa.org/videos).

Person-centered psychotherapy was the first truly American theory of psychotherapy, and as such created a monumental change in the actual practice of psychotherapy. As one of the most influential and revered psychologists, Carl Rogers developed this model rooted in principles of democracy and humanism, believing that people were best served when they were helped to find their own best way. Though Carl Rogers is synonymous with the person-centered approach, the theory has evolved over time in response to changes in the field. In *Person-Centered Psychotherapies*, Dr. David J. Cain clearly presents the evolution and essential components of this core approach to contemporary clinical practice. He highlights the extensive clinical research supporting the efficacy of person-centered practice and provides illustrative case examples that depict this model in action. Because of the widespread adoption of this model by practitioners and training programs alike, *Person-Centered Psychotherapies* is an important addition to the series.

—Jon Carlson and Matt Englar-Carlson

REFERENCES

Frew, J., & Spiegler, M. (2008). *Contemporary psychotherapies for a diverse world.* Boston, MA: Lahaska Press.

Haley, J. (1997). *Leaving home: The therapy of disturbed young people.* New York, NY: Routledge.

Person-Centered Psychotherapies

1

Introduction

Carl Rogers's seminal ideas have had a pervasive, profound, and revolutionary effect on how psychotherapy has been conceived and practiced for the last 70 years. In a survey of clinical and counseling psychologists published in 1982 in *American Psychologist* (Smith, 1982), Rogers (1902–1987) was identified as the most influential psychotherapist. Twenty-five years later, in a much larger survey of psychotherapists conducted by *The Psychotherapy Networker* ("The Top 10," 2007), Rogers was again identified as the "most influential therapist" despite the fact that relatively few persons in the United States identify themselves as person-centered therapists. His foundational ideas, especially the significance of the therapeutic relationship as a means to growth, have been absorbed by many diverse approaches to psychotherapy. Person-centered therapy is based on the assumption that all humans have an innate tendency to actualize their potential to grow psychologically and to manage their lives effectively if provided a therapeutic relationship characterized by specific therapist qualities or conditions. This optimistic view of the client's potential for growth stood in stark contrast to Freud's darker view of the human psyche. Person-centered therapists believe that if their clients perceive that their therapists (a) understand who they are and how they perceive the world (empathic understanding), (b) accept them without judgment (unconditional positive regard), and (c) are genuine in the therapeutic relationship (congruence), then constructive therapeutic change is likely to take place. The fundamental endeavor of person-centered therapists is to establish these relational conditions for their clients.

The name given to the therapy that Rogers developed evolved over time. Initially his approach was called *non-directive psychotherapy* during the early to mid-1940s, emphasizing Rogers's belief that clients rather than therapists should determine the direction of therapy and that clients' autonomy in deciding how to live their lives should be respected and preserved. Person-centered therapists believe that optimal change and growth occurs when it is self-directed, as opposed to therapist-directed. Thus, clients determine the content of therapy, what directions they want their life to take and the means of achieving desired changes.

By the mid-1940s, Rogers called his approach *client-centered therapy,* a designation that persisted until the 1970s when he began to use the term *person-centered therapy.* Today *person-centered therapy* is most commonly used and is essentially synonymous with *client-centered therapy.* I will primarily use the term *person-centered therapy* throughout the text unless the earlier term *client-centered therapy* is relevant in a historical context.

Rogers's influence on American psychotherapy is enormous, though often indirect. More than any other therapist, Carl Rogers taught us to listen with sensitivity and to communicate that understanding to the client for further processing and personal learning. This desire to hear another person as he or she shares something of personal relevance is at the heart of all good therapy and caring relationships. All persons have a powerful and near-universal need to be heard, seen, accepted, and appreciated as they are, including their flaws and limitations. Conversely, clients often feel frustrated, discouraged, and alienated when misunderstood or judged by their therapists and others who matter to them. People are naturally drawn to those who listen with compassion and acceptance. Whether they are therapists, teachers, parents, family members, coaches, employers, leaders, friends, or others of personal importance, such confidants are critical to a person's well-being.

Rogers demonstrated that the quality of the therapist–client relationship, in itself, has the potential to foster personal learning and growth in the client. Many of our clients come to us with low self-esteem and interpersonal insecurities that have developed in damaging relationships with their parents, partners, and significant others. Such clients often need and benefit from a relationship in which their therapists' regard and valuing is unconditional. In order to repair their feelings of low self-worth, even self-loathing, clients often benefit from the prizing and affirmation of their therapists that assists them in revising their self-views in more accepting and positive directions. There are times when the quality and depth of contact itself seem to enable clients to experience themselves in new and, sometimes, transformative ways. Many persons have had powerful experiences with others who have made constructive and lasting impacts on their lives. Such experiences are often possible in moments of therapy during which there is a genuine meeting between therapist and client.

In addition to affirming the client, the quality of the therapist–client relationship almost always plays a critical role in the process of therapeutic learning. Clients are most likely to learn with and from therapists they value, like, trust, and perceive as having their best interests at heart. Conversely, clients' therapeutic progress is often impaired when they have negative or ambivalent feelings toward their therapists. Thus, a solid therapeutic relationship serves as the foundation upon which constructive learning takes place.

Rogers was a pioneer whose groundbreaking insights and discoveries continue to have far-reaching effects on the field of psychotherapy. Rogers and his students were the first to study the counseling process in depth. In 1940, with the assistance of Bernie Covner, the first audio readings of a therapy session were made on 78-rpm recordings. These "live" and transcribed recordings provided moment-to-moment understandings of the therapeutic process and its immediate effects on the client as well as case studies for training and research. The case of Herbert Bryan (Rogers, 1942) was the first phonographically recorded verbatim transcript of an entire course of psychotherapy ever published. Although today we take for granted the usefulness of reviewing audio and video recordings for training purposes,

Rogers was the first to demystify psychotherapy by bringing it out into the open for study. Rogers was also a pioneer in carrying out and publishing psychotherapy research studies and was primarily responsible for initiating research in the field of psychotherapy. In 1957 he articulated a bold hypothesis regarding the "Necessary and Sufficient Conditions of Therapeutic Personality Change." This simple and elegant statement has probably generated more research than any other therapeutic hypothesis in the field. The research tradition established by Rogers and his students has carried forward to the present to ensure the continued development and efficacy of client-centered therapy. In 1959, Rogers published his magnum opus, "A Theory of Therapy, Personality, and Interpersonal Relationships," which remains as the most formal statement of person-centered theory. However, Rogers's theory has not remained static as many person-centered scholars and practitioners have continued to expand and modify this seminal approach. Rogers himself always supported and encouraged continuing developments in theory and practice and firmly believed that his approach should continue to evolve. Today, there is no longer one version of person-centered therapy but a number of continuously evolving approaches to therapy.

Rogers has been characterized as a quiet revolutionary because his ideas issued a fundamental challenge to other therapeutic approaches, especially those embracing a medical model that views the therapist's role as primary in diagnosing the client's problem and deciding on an appropriate course of therapy to treat a specific form of psychopathology. Rogers's use of the term *client* instead of *patient* conveys his belief that persons in therapy are capable and resourceful, not sick, helpless, or in need of guidance. Psychopathology or problems in living were understood as the client's ineffective attempt to cope with problems as opposed to a defect or deficiency. As is suggested by the descriptors "nondirective" and "client-centered," Rogers placed the client at the center of the change process and relied on the client's resources and potential for constructive change. The therapist's role was one of freeing clients to explore themselves and their lived experiences and to help them release or realize their inherent tendency for growth. Rogers's radical views continue to serve as a challenge and alternate view of how psychotherapy is conceived and practiced.

An enormous body of research conducted over a period of 70 years supports the effectiveness of person-centered psychotherapies. This research is ongoing and continues to generate new hypotheses and assess various aspects of person-centered psychotherapies, resulting in an increasingly expanded and refined understanding of the effective processes of therapy. It includes both quantitative and qualitative methods designed to understand the inner experiences of therapist and client as well as the effectiveness of person-centered therapy with a number of specific forms of psychopathology.

Person-centered psychotherapies are thriving all over the world. Kirschenbaum and Jourdan (2005) reported that between 1987 and 2004, a total of 777 person-centered publications, including 141 books, were published. This total far exceeds all of the previous publications over a 40-year period from 1946 to 1986. Further, there are approximately 200 person-centered organizations and training centers worldwide. In most graduate programs in psychology and counseling, students are trained in empathic responding and relational skills as a foundation for most therapeutic approaches. Recent years have seen many developments in theory and refinements in practice, thereby broadening the effectiveness of person-centered therapy. Clearly, the person-centered approach is alive and well and continues to have an enormous impact on the practice of many, if not most, therapists. In sum, person-centered therapy is as vital and relevant as it has ever been and continues to develop in ways that will make it increasingly so in the years to come. Finally, in a time when the world seems increasingly dehumanized by many forces, the humanizing message and effects of person-centered therapies are sorely needed.

2

History

The roots of client-centered therapy reach back to the late 1920s when Carl Rogers spent his formative years as a clinical psychologist in Rochester, New York. Rogers was a pragmatist in practice. As he found himself faced with large numbers of troubled children and parents, his guiding questions were "Does it work?" and "Is it effective?"

Rogers's approach to his clinical work was based on careful systematic observation as opposed to trial and error. Not content to rely on subjective impressions, he carefully evaluated the effects of his work. This would become a lifetime endeavor and strong value.

During his Rochester years (1928–1939), Rogers came to believe that "most children, if given a reasonably normal environment which meets their own emotional, intellectual and social needs, have within themselves sufficient drive toward health to respond and make a comfortable adjustment to life" (Kirschenbaum, 1979, p. 75). An important belief emerging in Rogers's practice was the notion that individual growth was more likely to occur in a certain kind of interpersonal environment.

While he experimented with a number of treatment approaches, including psychoanalytic, Rogers came to find each one lacking in some way. Ever a pragmatist, he abandoned any approach that did not seem effective. After several years of experience working with troubled children and their parents, Rogers began to realize that he was "moving away from any approach which was coercive or strongly interpretative, not for philosophical reasons, but because such approaches were never more than superficially effective" (Burton, 1972, pp. 47–48).

Around 1936, Rogers became interested in Otto Rank's work and invited Rank to Rochester for a weekend seminar, which Rogers described as "very profitable." About the Rankian approach Rogers recalled, " its major value may be . . . the fresh viewpoint of non-interference and reliance on the individual's own tendency toward growth" (Kirschenbaum, 1979, p. 93). Rogers was also drawn to Rank's emphasis on the therapist's supportive and acceptant stance toward the client and the value placed on client self-insight. Rogers embraced four specific elements of Rank's relational therapy: (a) the importance of the quality of relationship between therapist and client, (b) the therapist's endeavor to provide an atmosphere that enables clients to "experience and realize" their own attitudes, (c) the therapist's acceptance of the client and a disinclination to impose recommendations or viewpoints on clients, and (d) an emphasis on clarification of the client's feelings and acceptance of the client.

Toward the end of his Rochester years, Rogers identified in his first book, *The Clinical Treatment of the Problem Child* (1939), some of the basic elements that would form the foundation for what would be later known as client-centered therapy. These elements consisted of a sympathetic understanding, respect for the individual, and an understanding of the self of the client.

OHIO STATE UNIVERSITY (1939–1945)

Rogers left Rochester and took a position at Ohio State University in 1939 as a full professor in the psychology department. In addition to teaching a full load of courses, he supervised counseling students, wrote several articles, and counseled several students. Rogers established a practicum in counseling and psychotherapy in 1940 for graduate trainees that was likely the first such supervised training offered in a university setting.

While at Ohio State, Rogers wrote *Counseling and Psychotherapy: Newer Concepts in Practice* (1942), a classic textbook on basic therapeutic issues, methods, the therapy relationship, and the process of change. The descriptive terms *non-directive* and *client* were introduced to underscore the therapist's belief that the direction and locus of control in therapy were clearly centered in the person seeking help. This was a radical shift away from the interpretive and directive methods that were commonly employed at the time. As Seeman perceptively stated, "The enduring process which Rogers set in motion in 1942 was a reexamination of the nature of therapy . . . which continues to this day" (Wolman, 1965, p. 1215).

Rogers and his students were the first to study the counseling process in depth, assisted in large part by audio recordings of therapy sessions. These "live" and transcribed recordings proved invaluable as resources for both training and research. Finally, Rogers was a pioneer in carrying out and publishing research studies in counseling. Early in *Counseling and Psychotherapy,* Rogers stated that the book "endeavors to formulate a definite and understandable series of hypotheses . . . which may be tested and explored" (pp. 16–17). The research tradition established by Rogers and his students during this period has carried forward to the present to ensure the continued development and efficacy of person-centered therapy.

UNIVERSITY OF CHICAGO (1945–1957)

In 1945 Rogers left Ohio State to create and direct the Counseling Center at the University of Chicago. There he continued to develop client-centered theory and practice while conducting research on its effectiveness. Rogers said about his Chicago years that this was "a period in which our basic views about the helping relationship came to fruition. . . . It was a germinal period for research hypotheses and theoretical formulations" (Burton, 1972, p. 54).

In 1951, Rogers's third major book, *Client-Centered Therapy,* was published. Applications of the client-centered approach to play therapy, group therapy, leadership and administration, teaching, and counselor training were advanced. In this period, Rogers further emphasized the attitudes of the therapist as primary over technique, as well as the capacity of the client for constructive change. Rogers focused on creating a relationship that would release the client's natural tendency for actualization and growth. Increasing emphasis was placed on understanding the client's phenomenal world and its meaning.

Between 1943 and 1957, approximately 200 studies were conducted on client-centered therapy and its applications to children, groups, education, industry, and leadership. In 1954, the results of a group of studies, co-edited by Rogers and Rosalind Dymond, were published in *Psychotherapy and Personality Change*. The studies that Rogers referred to as a "pioneering venture" were moderately supportive of client-centered hypotheses.

Rogers received considerable credit and praise for the research efforts he stimulated at the Counseling Center. Joseph Matarrazzo placed Rogers's research efforts in perspective in 1965 when he wrote: "His approach to the interview stimulated research more than the works of any single writer on the interview before or since"; Matarrazzo went on to state that *Psychotherapy and Personality Change* was "probably the single most important research publication on interviewing (as found in psychotherapy) of the decade" (Kirschenbaum, 1979, p. 219). Based primarily on his research contributions in psychotherapy, Rogers, along with Kenneth W. Spence and Wolfgang Kohler, was awarded the first Distinguished Scientific Contribution Award presented by the American Psychological Association in 1956.

In 1957, Rogers published his formulation of what he would call "The Necessary and Sufficient Conditions of Therapeutic Personality Change." This formulation represented the culmination of many years of development in his thinking.

UNIVERSITY OF WISCONSIN (1957–1963)

In the spring of 1957, Rogers accepted a position at the University of Wisconsin, much to the chagrin of the University of Chicago Counseling Center staff who were stunned by his sudden decision to leave. Rogers and his colleagues were curious to see if his hypothesis about the necessary and sufficient conditions of personality change applied to seriously disturbed persons. In 1957 he began to develop an ambitious research project on the treatment of persons suffering from schizophrenia. The results of the study showed no significant differences between the therapy group and the control group, although there was a correlation between high levels of the therapist conditions of congruence and empathy and successful outcome. While much was learned about psychotherapy with schizophrenic persons, the research evidence for client-centered therapy was modest.

In 1959, Rogers published "A Theory of Therapy, Personality and Interpersonal Relationships" in Sigmund Koch's *Psychology: A Study of a Science*. This 72-page formal statement of his theory continues to stand as the most complete articulation of Rogers's position. Rogers's fifth major book, *On Becoming a Person*, was published in 1961. It contains many of his best-known and most influential papers. Some of his most provocative and incisive thinking on psychotherapy, education research, philosophy of science, interpersonal relations, family life, creativity, the process of growth, and the fully functioning person are contained in this book. Soon after its publication, there was an enormous outpouring of touching and appreciative responses from professionals and laypersons from every walk of life. Rogers's humane and provocative message had clearly struck a chord.

LA JOLLA AND CENTER FOR STUDIES OF THE PERSON (1964–1987)

In the summer of 1963, Rogers resigned from the University of Wisconsin and moved to California, in part because of the harsh way he felt graduate students were being treated. For several years, starting in 1964, Rogers involved himself in the encounter group movement and became a national leader in the field. The magazine *Psychology Today* identified him as a "grand master" while *Look* magazine referred to him as "an elder statesman of encounter groups." In 1970, Rogers completed *Carl Rogers on Encounter Groups*, which clearly associated him with encounter groups among both professionals and the general public. In 1972, Rogers received the first Distinguished Professional Contribution Award from the American Psychological Association.

During the 1970s, a modest approach to family therapy was presented by Raskin and van der Veen, while Tom Gordon was developing a program for parent effectiveness training (P.E.T), which would eventually impact millions of parents and children worldwide. In sum, the 1960s and 1970s were a fertile period of development in the theory and practice of therapy and the expansion of client-centered concepts into diverse areas of application.

In the last 15 or so years of his life, Rogers became increasingly interested in broader social issues, especially peace. Beginning in 1974, Carl and his daughter, Natalie Rogers, along with several of their colleagues, initiated a series of large group workshops, sometimes 2 or 3 weeks in length, to explore the implications of the person-centered approach for building optimal communities in groups ranging from 75 to 800 persons. For the first time, Rogers would use the phrase *person-centered* to describe these workshops, which would be offered all over the world for the next several years. As those workshops evolved, Rogers and the staff of facilitators provided less and less structure, instead leaving most, if not all, of the decision making to the entire community. Such large community groups are rarely part of person-centered practice today. Their demise was primarily because they were often frustrating and contentious and had relatively little demonstrated therapeutic value.

A Way of Being was published in 1980. It is a diverse collection of papers representing the evolution of Rogers's thought in the 1970s. Many of the papers were very personal statements of Rogers' growth and changing views.

In 1986 the quarterly academic journal *Person-Centered Review* began publication under the editorship of this author. Up to this point Rogers had discouraged the creation of client-centered training programs, organizations, or journals, fearing that his approach would become formalized and dogmatic. By 1986, however, Rogers supported and welcomed the journal and wrote in its first issue that it "will help to tie together the global network that already exists but lacks awareness of itself. The *Review* can be a vehicle for new ideas, innovative methods, thoughtful critiques, new models of research, and integrative philosophical and theoretical thinking" (Rogers, 1986, p. 5).

Unfortunately, Carl Rogers was not able to pursue further the strongest commitments of his last years—to contribute whatever he could to the prevention of nuclear war and the achievement of world peace. On January 20, 1987, on the day when Rogers fell and broke his hip and required hospitalization, he was nominated, at age 85, by Congressman Jim Bates for the 1987 Nobel Peace Prize. A few weeks later, on February 4, 1987, Rogers died as he had hoped he would—with his boots on and, as always, looking forward. He had been relatively healthy and active until his death.

From the time of Rogers's death, there has been a substantial amount of progress in the theory and practice in person-centered theory. In the next chapter, I will review Rogers's basic theory as well as recent developments.

3

Theory

Carl Rogers published the most complete statement of his approach in 1959 and never modified it in any significant way. However, Rogers never considered his theory to be a finished product and anticipated that it would be developed further over time. The most essential concepts of his approach will be identified in this section, followed by variations of person-centered therapy and substantive contemporary developments

THERAPEUTIC GOALS

The goals of the person-centered therapist are primarily process goals. Therefore, the quality of engagement, moment to moment, between therapist and client is central. The fundamental goal of person-centered therapists is the creation of an optimal therapeutic relationship for their clients. As Rogers has eloquently stated: "Individuals have within themselves vast resources for self-understanding, and for altering their self-concepts, basic attitudes, and self-directed behavior; these resources can be tapped if a definable climate of facilitative psychological attitudes can be provided" (1980, p. 115). The "definable climate" includes (a) the therapist's congruence, genuineness, authenticity, or transparency;

(b) unconditional positive regard or nonpossessive warmth, acceptance, nonjudgmental caring, liking, prizing, affirmation; and (c) a genuine desire to understand the client's experience and accurate empathic communication of that experience. Toward the end of his life, Rogers also identified therapist *presence* as a powerful and facilitative aspect of the person-centered therapist's manner of being. Rogers (1957) assumed that if the client experienced these therapist qualities or conditions, personal growth would take place.

While Rogers and other person-centered therapists were concerned with clients' achievement of their goals, the emphasis of the therapist is on creating conditions for growth rather than alleviation of symptoms alone. In other words, the emphasis is on the development of the whole person rather than on a specific complaint. For some person-centered therapists, the only goal is to provide the core conditions while other person-centered therapists believe that the identification of and focus on specific client-generated goals is desirable because it gives the therapy direction and cohesion and assures that the therapist and client are working toward the client's ends.

KEY CONCEPTS
Actualizing Tendency

Rogers defined the *actualizing tendency* as "the inherent tendency of the organism to develop all its capacities in ways which serve to maintain or enhance the organism" (1959, p.196). This definition suggests that people naturally move toward differentiation, expansion in growth, wholeness, integration, autonomy and self-regulation, and effectiveness in functioning. The actualizing tendency is viewed as a biologically based master motive that subsumes other motives such as a reduction in needs, tensions, and drives as well as an inclination to learn and be creative. It is the bedrock on which person-centered psychotherapy is based. A core belief in an actualizing tendency is the basis for the client-centered therapist's trust and optimism in clients' resourcefulness and capacity to move forward and find solutions to their problems. Art Combs, speaking of the person's fundamental drive toward fulfillment or health stated, "clients can, will and *must* move toward health, *if* the way seems open to them to do so" (1999, p.8, italics in original). Tageson believes that the "living organism . . . will always do the best it can to actualize its potentials . . . and it will do so as a *unit* along all dimensions of its functioning" (1982, p.35, italics in original). While Rogers viewed the actualizing tendency as primarily constructive and prosocial, he and others (e.g., Bohart, 2007) acknowledged that persons may develop behaviors that are neither moral nor enhancing though they represent persons' attempt to adapt as best they can (e.g., lying or stealing to get something one wants). Although life experiences may weaken the actualizing tendency, it is always assumed to exist as a potential on which clients can draw.

Self, Ideal Self, and Self-Actualization

The *self* (self-concept, self-structure) as defined by Rogers (1959) is the "organized, consistent conceptual gestalt composed of perceptions of characteristics of the 'I' or 'me'. . . together with the values attached to these perceptions"(p. 200). The self is a fluid and changing gestalt that is available to awareness and that is definable at a given time. Though relatively consistent over time, it is also malleable as new experiences alter the ways persons view themselves. The terms *self* or *self-concept* represent persons' views of who they are, while the term *self-structure* represents an external view of the self. The *ideal self* represents the view of self the person would like to be. Often there is a discrepancy between the self one sees oneself to be and the person one hopes or strives to be.

As the self-structure is developed, the "general tendency toward actualization expresses itself also in the actualization of that portion of the experience of the organism which is symbolized in the self" (Rogers, 1959, p. 196). Thus, when aspects of experience defined as the self are actualized (e.g., "I am athletic"), the process is one of *self-actualization*. The actualization of the self may be in harmony with the actualizing tendency to maintain and enhance the organism, or it may be at odds with the actualizing tendency, resulting in the development of aspects of the self that may be valued by the person but have adverse consequences. For example, the person may develop his or her capacity to be deceptive, thus gaining desired ends from others while such deception compromises the integrity of the person and therefore does not maintain or enhance the total organism/person.

Congruence and Incongruence

Congruence describes a state in which the person's self-concept and experiences, including thoughts, feelings, and behavior, are in harmony. That is, the person is integrated, whole, or genuine. Rogers believed that congruence represents an optimal state of functioning and a primary quality of mental health. *Incongruence* represents a state of discord between the self-concept and experience. Rogers (1959) described this state as one of "tension and internal confusion" (p. 203) because people cannot reconcile the discrepancy between their thoughts, feelings, or actions and the way they perceive themselves. For example, a person who views himself or herself as having high integrity will likely experience distress when realizing that he or she frequently engages in dishonest behavior. When a person is in a state of incongruence but is unaware of it, the person becomes vulnerable to experiencing anxiety, threat, and disorganization or confusion about the sense of self. At such moments the person may feel a wave of uncertainty or insecurity about who they are and experience being out of sorts, troubled by some vague concern, or "off center."

Psychological Adjustment and Maladjustment

In Rogers's theory, optimal *psychological adjustment* "exists when the concept of the self is such that all experiences are or may be assimilated on a symbolic level into the gestalt of the self-structure. Optimal psychological adjustment is thus synonymous with complete congruence of self and experience, or complete openness to experience" (1959, p. 206). Rogers believed that if persons were nondefensively receptive to all experiences, they would likely make good decisions, achieve high levels of adjustment, and function well. In short, a person who is psychologically adjusted is congruent and integrated and functions well because he or she has taken in and assessed all experiences and information that may be relevant to living effectively.

On the other hand, "*psychological maladjustment* exists when the organism denies to awareness, or distorts in awareness, significant experiences, which consequently are not accurately symbolized and organized into the gestalt of the self-structure, thus creating an incongruence between self and experience" (Rogers, 1959, p. 204). Thus, maladaption is essentially a state of incongruence between one's self and one's experience. The person is likely to experience *threat* when "an experience is perceived . . . as incongruent with the structure of the self" (p. 204). Consequently, the person cannot integrate some experiences or corresponding actions with the self because they don't fit. For example, a man confidently entering a talent show (seeing himself as talented) may get feedback from credible judges that he has little or no talent. The person is thrown into a state of threat and disillusionment because he cannot reconcile the disheartening feedback with a view of himself as talented. He may be inclined to deny or distort such threatening information in an attempt to maintain the integrity of the self as perceived. Thus, after a period of time, the man who received feedback that he was not talented may revise the view of self by denying that the judges were fair or competent in perceiving the person's "real" talent. By doing so, he remains maladjusted because his decisions are based on incomplete or distorted information.

Experience and Openness to Experience

By *experience*, Rogers referred to

> all that is going on within the envelope of the organism at any given moment which is potentially available to awareness. It includes events of which the individual is unaware, as well as all the phenomena which are in consciousness. . . . It includes the influence of memory and past experience, as these are active in the moment, in restricting or broadening the meaning given to various stimuli. It also includes all that is present in immediate awareness or consciousness. (1959, p. 197)

Experience includes the person's awareness of his or her behavior. Synonyms include the *experiential field* and *phenomenal field,* and this concept encompasses thoughts, feelings, sensations, and images.

When the person is *open to experience*, he or she readily takes in information arising from within or from the external environment without defensiveness. Openness to experience is critical to optimal functioning because it enables the person to receive and process any and all experiences and draw from those experiences to make effective decisions in daily life. Conversely, defensiveness reduces the person's receptivity to experience, capacity to process, make sense of, and act on experience that may be threatening to the self. Simply put, sometimes what one may benefit from knowing is not necessarily what one may be willing or able to know and examine. A woman who makes excuses for her boyfriend's failure to make time for her or show much interest in her may be failing to access information critical to her dealing effectively with him. Failing to do so renders her vulnerable to self-blame, insecurity, anxiety, or depression.

Positive Regard and Unconditional Positive Regard

People experience *positive regard* when they perceive that some aspect of their self-experience (e.g., feelings, beliefs) or behavior makes a positive difference to or is valued by someone else. In this state the person is likely to feel warmth, liking, respect, and acceptance from others. Rogers (1959) views the need for positive regard as a basic need that is essential to one's well-being. We experience *unconditional positive regard* when we perceive that any experience or behavior is accepted without conditions by another person. Thus, a person may act in ways of which he or she is not proud but still find that he or she is accepted by another. Rogers (1959) states, "This means to value the person, irrespective of the differential values which one may place on his specific behaviors" (p. 208). When clients experience unconditional positive regard from their therapists, they are likely to feel accepted and prized, which in turn enables them to develop more tolerant and accepting feelings toward themselves. While unconditional positive regard is theoretically possible, some have argued that it is an unachievable ideal. However, when clients feel predominantly accepted and consistently valued for who they are by their therapists or significant others, they are likely to develop positive and accepting views of themselves. This desire to be seen accurately and be accepted seems to be a powerful and universal need in people. Therapists display unconditional positive regard toward their clients when they are accepting toward experiences or behaviors of which clients may sometimes be proud and, at other times, ashamed. Consequently, clients learn to accept themselves as flawed but worthy persons.

Clients experience *positive self-regard* when they are accepting of their behavior independently of whether the behavior is accepted or prized by others. *Unconditional self-regard* is experienced when an "individual perceives himself in such a way that no self-experience can be discriminated as more or less worthy of positive regard than any other" (Rogers, 1959, p. 209). That is, the person continues to value himself or herself regardless of his or her experiences or behavior. Again, while unconditional self-regard is theoretically possible, it is more likely that persons generally accept themselves while being aware they sometimes fail to live up to their own standards.

Conditions of Worth

Conditions of worth exist in the person "when a self-experience . . . is either avoided or sought solely because the individual discriminates it as being less or more worthy of self-regard" (Rogers, 1959, p. 209). Simply put, this means that an individual may engage in or avoid a behavior based on whether it brings him or her acceptance or regard from another person. The approval of another may take on such importance that the person disregards whether or not the behavior enhances his or her self, growth, or well-being. Children are especially vulnerable to the conditions of worth communicated by their parents and significant others and therefore may value an experience or behavior "positively or negatively solely because of these conditions of worth which he has taken over from others, not because the experience enhances or fails to enhance his organism" (p. 209). Consequently, an experience "may be perceived as organismically satisfying, when in fact this is not true" (p. 210). For example, a young boy may be proud that he does not cry when he is hurt because he has learned from his parents that crying is weak while stifling one's tears means he is a "big boy." If his parents did not disapprove of crying, the boy would likely cry when distressed and experience this behavior as natural and acceptable.

As primarily social beings, people are constantly concerned about how others see them and whether others like or approve of them. Consequently, most people engage in frequent "image management" to achieve other's approval and whatever benefits accompany such approval. The dilemma of image management and approval seeking is that, even though people may avoid rejection by important others, they become alienated from themselves and fearful of being the natural, spontaneous selves they are. Internally, they know they are not being true to themselves and sometimes feel like frauds. However, this need to be liked and accepted can be so powerful as to compromise one's values, integrity, and self. It does indeed take courage to be and reveal one's true self since the risks of disapproval and rejection may be real. Conversely, living authentically and being true to one's self brings the satisfaction that comes from standing somewhere for something. It enables one to live with integrity even though it may create discord with others. As Rogers has said, "it's risky to live."

Locus of Evaluation

Locus of evaluation refers to the source of the person's values. If the source is internal, the person is "the center of the valuing process, the evidence being supplied by his own senses. When the locus of evaluation resides in others, their judgment as to the value of an . . . experience becomes the criterion of value for the individual" (Rogers, 1959, p. 209). Rogers viewed functioning from an internal locus of evaluation as a sign of autonomy or self-governance and mental health. When the locus of evaluation is external, the person relies on the views of others, especially persons of authority or other authoritative sources (e.g., Bible, parents) to guide their lives. People often prefer to allow others to guide or influence their choices in hope that it will lead to a sound and safe decision while removing full responsibility from themselves for their decisions (e.g., "I followed the advice of my therapist"). Conversely, making choices based on one's own beliefs, values, and senses may be experienced as more risky but may also result in a feeling of pride, confidence, and self-reliance.

Organismic Valuing Process

This process suggests that persons have a built-in, trustworthy, evaluative mechanism that enables them to experience "satisfaction in those . . . behaviors which maintain and enhance the organism and the self" (Rogers, 1959, p. 209). As an ongoing process, experiences are viewed freshly and valued in terms of how well they serve the person's sense of well-being and potential growth. Person-centered therapists' belief in the organismic valuing process enables them to trust that clients will act in their best interests when guided by this bodily felt source of wisdom. Consequently, person-centered therapists facilitate the client's attending to all experiences, external and internal, to guide them. For persons to benefit from the guidance and wisdom of their organismic valuing processes, they must pay attention to their inner voices, feelings, and intuitions and discriminate which of these is likely to enhance their choices for healthy living. Clients, of course, may choose to ignore the inherent wisdom of their organismic valuing processes and make life decisions based on other factors that they perceive to serve them at a given time. For example, a wife's allegiance to her abusing spouse may be harmful to her well-being and growth but chosen nevertheless because the spouse provides for her basic needs (e.g., food and dwelling) and even some of her emotional needs (e.g., periodic love and affection).

Internal and External Frame of Reference

The client's *internal frame of reference* refers to "all of the realm of experience which is available to the awareness of the individual at a given moment" (Rogers, 1959, p. 209). It is the subjective experience of the person and can only be known fully by the person. This frame of reference includes thoughts, feelings, perceptions, sensations, meanings, memories, and fantasies. Therapist empathy enables the therapist to grasp the client's inner world through inference, though the accuracy of the therapist's understanding is confirmed or disconfirmed by the client. To view another person from an *external frame of reference* means to "perceive solely from one's own subjective internal frame of reference without empathizing with the observed person" (1959, p. 211). For example, a man who spends long hours at work each day may perceive himself as dedicated to his family (internal frame of reference), while his wife may view him as neglecting his family (external frame of reference).

Empathy

Empathy exists when one person accurately perceives "the internal frame of reference of another with accuracy, and with the emotional components and meanings which pertain thereto, as if one were the other person, but without ever losing the 'as if' condition" (1959, p. 210). In person-centered therapy, empathy is considered to be a capacity for understanding another, a desirable attitude and a response that communicates understanding that enables clients to clarify, process, and learn from their experiences. Empathy is one of the primary means by which we bridge over to other persons and grasp their worldviews and realities. Empathy involves the use our imagination and powers of inference to grasp what it is like to be that other person in that person's current life space and context. When person-centered therapists attempt to grasp and communicate their clients' subjective realities, both therapist and client engage in a mutual process of refinement of the client's experience that typically proceeds until the client senses and confirms the truthfulness of the understanding. In this sense, the process is one of collaborative empathy in which the client's truth is cocreated.

THEORY OF PERSONALITY

Rogers developed a rudimentary theory of psychological development and personality that was derived primarily from his observations of the therapeutic process. Summarized and paraphrased below in a condensed form are the main concepts of his theory.

Postulated Characteristics of the Human Infant

Rogers believed that infants perceive their experience as reality. Thus, their perception forms the basis of the reality with which they engage since they have only this perspective to relate to, as opposed to some "actual" reality. Infants have an inherent motivational system, an actualizing tendency that propels them to maintain themselves and develop their potential. The infant's behavior can be understood as his or her attempt to satisfy needs for actualization in his or her perceived reality. The infant's organismic valuing process orients him or her to value and pursue experiences that maintain and enhance his or her development and functioning. Thus, the infant is likely to move toward experiences that help him or her thrive while avoiding those that seem adverse to his or her well-being.

As the infant develops, the child becomes more differentiated and complex and begins to become aware of being a separate self as he or she interacts with significant others (e.g., mother) in his or her environment. A rudimentary concept of self is developed that will be elaborated, refined, and clarified over time. As awareness of self emerges, the infant develops a need for positive regard, which is seen as universal and continuous throughout life. His or her satisfaction depends on how the infant perceives others' attitudes and behaviors toward himself or herself. The infant experiences positive regard when he or she perceives that he or she is valued by others and when perceiving himself or herself as satisfying another's need for self-regard. For example, when the infant smiles and receives a hug from her mother, she experiences positive regard. When an infant satisfies his mother's need for self-regard (e.g., the infant hugs his mother when picked up), he also experiences positive regard. In other words, there is a reciprocal positive effect of affectionate behavior on the infant's and mother's feelings of worth. At times, the need for positive regard from significant others may be more compelling than the organismic valuing process and experiences that actualize the individual. For example, the infant may acquiesce to her mother's command to "stop banging on the piano," an activity she finds stimulating and pleasurable, deciding that it is more important to please her mother than to satisfy her own desires. Projected into childhood and adulthood, sometimes the desire for approval and positive regard from others becomes more compelling than the person's natural inclination to actualize himself or herself. Over time, self-experiences of the person may come to be experienced independently of the positive regard of others as self-regard. Thus, persons learn to regard themselves in a negative or positive manner based on their own assessments of others' responses to them, their experiences, and behavior. Consequently, persons may view themselves with more or less regard than others observing the same behavior. For example, a college sprinter coming in second in a field of 10 runners in a 100-meter race may experience "failure" while that person's coach holds the runner in higher regard for his or her performance. Persons with low self-esteem often have lower regard for themselves than most of their peers, while persons who tend to be narcissistic hold themselves in higher esteem than their peers.

As persons develop, they learn that significant others in their lives value some of their behaviors and experiences while disapproving of others. That is, others become conditional in their regard. For example, a father disapproves of his son when he fails to eat all of the food on his plate but approves of him when he eats every bite. The son experiences conditions of worth from his father and learns over time that others, in general, will value or approve of him or not depending on whether he meets their standards for behavior. Clients in therapy are often plagued as adults by powerful needs for approval from their parents or other important persons in their lives. Consequently, they seek that approval at the expense of their self-regard. When person-centered therapy is effective, such clients learn to regard themselves in a positive manner despite the disapproval that may come from others.

Individuals develop their own conditions of worth for self-regard as they develop. Thus, it is inevitable that some behaviors will be viewed as reflecting positively on the person while others will be viewed as reflectively negatively on him or her. Because all persons have a need for self-regard, they may engage in a form of self-deception in which some behaviors (e.g., deception) are justified (e.g., "he would be upset by the truth") in order to maintain positive self-regard. However, at some level of awareness, the person recognizes that some behaviors do not fit with a positive view of self. At such times the person experiences a sense of discomfort and threat to the self as perceived (e.g., honest and trustworthy) and experiences a state of incongruence since the perceived self is at variance with the person's behavior. Consequently, the person is faced with revising the view of self (e.g., "I am sometimes deceptive") or distorting experiences in a manner that results in his or her becoming estranged by self-deception in an attempt to maintain self-regard (e.g., "my deception is justified").

Threats to the self can be extremely disruptive and anxiety provoking, casting people into a state of uncertainty and confusion about who they are. When some aspects of behavior are accurately perceived (e.g., "I sometimes deceive others for personal ends"), the current view of self (as honest) can no longer be preserved and the person is faced with reconciling the discrepancy between his or her behavior and view of self. Therefore, self-regard is diminished or compromised since the person's conditions for self-worth have been violated. However, the person may engage his or her defenses to prevent aspects of behavior from being perceived accurately in an attempt to preserve the self as conceived. The consequence is that the person's ability to perceive accurately is reduced. If this perceptual distortion becomes substantial, it is likely that the person will experience increasing discomfort, confusion, and doubt about who he or she is, with a result that intrapersonal and interpersonal relations will be strained and impaired.

Therapy often helps the client become aware of such perceptual distortions (e.g., "I'm not the person I thought I was") and to revise the view of self in a manner compatible with the client's behavior. Revising the view of self is often an arduous process that requires courage on the part of the client. The therapist's empathic exploration and accepting attitude assists the client in re-evaluating and clarifying his or her view of self. Over time the client comes to accept previously distorted aspects of the self and integrates them into a more accurate view of the self (e.g., primarily honest but sometimes deceptive).

In the next section I will review the evolution of person-centered theory in psychotherapy, beginning with its initial forms in the 1940s and proceeding to the varieties of contemporary versions.

STAGES OF DEVELOPMENT OF PERSON-CENTERED PSYCHOTHERAPIES

I. Nondirective Psychotherapy (1940–1950)

When Rogers articulated the early version of his approach in 1942 in *Counseling and Psychotherapy*, the approach had a primarily technical emphasis. The therapist's main task was to reflect and clarify the client's message and feelings in an accepting manner. Strong emphasis was placed on the therapist's being nondirective, to distinguish this approach from interpretative (mostly psychoanalytic) and counselor-guided or directive therapies of the time. In a chapter entitled "The Directive Versus the Non-Directive Approach," Rogers made it clear that "the counselor takes no responsibility for directing the outcome of the process" (p. 115). He contrasted nondirective with directive counseling as follows:

> counseling of the directive sort is characterized by many highly specific questions to which specific answers are expected, and by information given by the counselor . . . [while] counseling of the non-directive sort is characterized by a preponderance of client activity. . . . The counselor's primary techniques are those which help the client more clearly to recognize and understand his feelings, attitudes and reaction patterns, and which encourage the client to talk about them. (1942, p. 124)

In his early stages of developing a "new" approach, a number of his proposals seemed to focus on what Rogers thought the therapist should *not* do or be. He was adamant in his belief that the therapist should not advise the client, interpret behavior, or attempt to direct or persuade the client to pursue a particular course of action. Rogers objected to these approaches because "they assume that the counselor is the one most competent to decide what are to be the goals of the individual, and what are the values by which the situation is to be judged" (1942, p. 27). Rogers believed that *counselor-centered therapy* "may serve only to make the counselee more dependent, less able to solve new problems of adjustment" (Kirschenbaum, 1979, p. 116), and more resistant to the counselor.

Rogers goes on to say that the "non-directive point of view places a high value on the right of every individual to be psychologically independent and to maintain his psychological integrity" (1942, p. 127).

Zimring and Raskin (1992) characterized the process of nondirective therapy as follows: "If the therapist accepts, recognizes and clarifies the feelings expressed by the client, there will be movement from negative feelings to positive ones, followed by insight and positive actions that will be initiated by the client" (p. 630).

Rogers made a major shift in emphasis in therapy by focusing on the *person* of the client rather than on the problem expressed. Another shift was toward the *feelings* expressed by the client as opposed to the client's thoughts. The therapist's *attitudes* of respect for and belief in the client's capacity for self-directed growth resulted in the development of a dramatically different kind of relationship with the client, one characterized by disciplined restraint and non-intrusiveness. The therapist as an individual stayed out of the relationship and instead attempted to be a careful, supportive, and *understanding listener*.

II. Client-Centered Therapy (1951–1960)

By the time *Client-Centered Therapy* was published in 1951, Rogers's approach shifted from an emphasis on therapist technique to a greater emphasis on the attitudes of the therapist and the subjective world of the client. He articulated 19 propositions that formed the basis of a rudimentary theory of personality and behavior. The propositions are summarized below.

1. Every individual exists in a continually changing world of experience of which he or she is the center.
2–3. The organism reacts to the field as it is experienced and perceived and reacts as a whole to this phenomenal field.
4. The organism has one basic tendency—to actualize, maintain, and enhance the organism.
5–6. Behavior is the goal-directed attempt of the organism to satisfy its needs as experienced, in the field as perceived, while emotion generally facilitates such goal-directed behavior.

7. The best vantage point for understanding behavior is from the internal frame of reference of the individual.

8–10. A portion of the total perceptual field gradually becomes differentiated as the self whose structure is an organized and fluid but consistent conceptual pattern of perceptions of the characteristics of "I" or "me," along with the values attached to the self.

11. Experiences are either symbolized or organized into some relationship to the self. They may be ignored because there is no perceived relationship to the self-structure, or symbolization may be denied or distorted because the experience is inconsistent with the self-structure.

12–13. Most of the organism's behaviors are consistent with the concept of self, while some behaviors may be brought about by experiences and needs that have not been symbolized and therefore may be inconsistent with the self-structure. Thus, they are not "owned" by the individual.

14–15. Psychological maladjustment exists when the organism denies significant experiences, which are not symbolized and organized into the self-structure, often leading to psychological tension. Conversely, psychological adjustment exists when experiences of the organism are assimilated into a consistent relationship with the concept of the self.

16–17. Experiences that are inconsistent with the self-structure may be experienced as a threat. During periods where there is no threat to the organism, experiences inconsistent with the self may be examined and assimilated into the self-structure.

18. When the individual perceives and accepts all experiences into a consistent and integrated system, the individual is more understanding and accepting of others as separate individuals.

19. As the individual accepts into his or her self-structure more of his or her organic experiences, the person replaces his or her present value system—based on introjects that have been distortedly symbolized—with a continuing organismic valuing process.

Rogers's 19 propositions show considerable advancement in theory from the initial nondirective period and formed the basis of his expanded and more formal statement of theory articulated in 1959. Arguably the most important concept articulated by Rogers was that of a pervasive motivational system, that of an actualizing tendency, which is the driving force in psychological development. If the person/organism is believed to have a natural tendency to maintain and enhance itself, then the therapist's task is to create interpersonal conditions for the client that enable the actualizing tendency to promote growth. Another substantial advance in theory was Rogers's view that a person reacts as a whole to the phenomenal field—that is, perception is the only reality to which the person can respond in the moment. This, of course, strongly points to the therapist's entering into and clarifying the perceptual/experiential field through empathic exploration of the client's internal or subjective frame of reference.

The articulation of a self or self-structure, the person's view of "I" or "me," was another major advance in theory. The self is viewed as both relatively consistent over time but sufficiently fluid to permit new experiences to alter the current view of self. Most of the person's behaviors would be consistent with the self-concept, while some would be experienced as discrepant and result in tension or threat.

Views of adjustment and maladjustment are also articulated. Rogers defined psychological adjustment in terms of the person's integration of experiences into a consistent relationship with the concept of the self. Conversely, maladjustment occurs when important experiences are not symbolized and integrated into the self-structure with a consequence that the person feels tension or discord.

Basic Therapeutic Hypothesis

In 1957 Rogers published a seminal paper entitled "The Necessary and Sufficient Conditions of Therapeutic Personality Change." His hypothesis is of the "if–then" variety, which means that "*if* certain conditions exist (independent variables), *then* a process (dependent variable) will occur which includes certain characteristic elements" (1959, p. 212, italics added). It states that for therapy to be effective, it is necessary that specific conditions exist:

1. Two persons are in psychological contact.
2. The first, whom we shall term the client, is in a state of incongruence, being vulnerable or anxious.

3. The second person, whom we shall term the therapist, is congruent or integrated in the relationship.
4. The therapist experiences unconditional positive regard for the client.
5. The therapist experiences an empathic understanding of the client's internal frame of reference and endeavors to communicate this experience to the client.
6. The communication to the client of the therapist's empathic understanding and unconditional positive regard is to a minimal degree achieved. (1957, p. 96)

Rogers later amended point 6 of this hypothesis by stating that the "therapist's genuineness (or congruence) must also be perceived by the client as well as his or her unconditional positive regard and empathic understanding" (Rogers & Stevens, 1967, p. 93). Surprisingly few modifications have been proposed to this hypothesis despite the fact that Rogers articulated it over 50 years ago.

Rogers's therapeutic experience led him to challenge the psychoanalytic concept of transference and the utility of diagnostic nomenclature. Rogers found that strong incidents of transference were relatively uncommon in client-centered therapy, though mild forms of transference attitudes (i.e., various feelings toward the therapist) were evident in most cases. Rogers believed that strong and prolonged transference relationships or "transference neuroses" were unlikely because the client-centered therapist's ongoing understanding and acceptance of all aspects of the client, including negative ones, lessened the possibility for intense transference. Transference reactions are also less likely to occur in person-centered therapy because therapists place a high value on being congruent and transparent with their clients, thereby lessening the likelihood that distorted reactions to therapists would occur.

Diagnosis or diagnostic categorization of the client was considered both unnecessary and counterproductive. Rogers especially objected to external diagnosis of the client by an "objective" expert. He believed that formal diagnosis was sometimes "detrimental or unwise" primarily because it may increase dependence in the client on the external authority of the therapist, resulting in the client losing confidence in his or her perceptions and concluding " I cannot know myself" (1951, p. 225). Rogers preferred to keep the locus of evaluation with the client, who then engages in an ongoing process of self-diagnosis or increased self-knowledge as an integral part of the therapeutic process.

III. On Becoming a Person (1961–1970)

In 1961, *On Becoming a Person* was published, marking further theoretical developments in client-centered therapy as well as expansions of applications in education, family life, group relations, and science. In therapy, the shift in emphasis was on the client's "becoming" or in Rogers's words "to be that self that one truly is." During this period Rogers articulated a view of what persons could become by describing the "fully functioning person." The characteristics of such a person included: (a) an increasing openness to experience, as opposed to defensiveness; (b) increasingly existential living, which implied a tendency to live fully and freshly in each moment; and (c) an increasing trust in one's organism, and especially one's feelings, as a means of living in the most satisfying way in various situations.

Many of Rogers's colleagues and other client/person-centered therapists were advancing fresh ideas in theory and research during this period. Eugene Gendlin, one of Rogers's colleagues, developed the concept of *experiencing,* an inner bodily sense of a problem to which the client could refer as a guide to self-*understanding and living in the moment.* Gendlin was one of the most creative of Rogers's colleagues and developed sophisticated methods to assist clients in focusing on and comprehending the meaning of their bodily felt experiences.

In 1970 Hart and Tomlinson published *New Directions in Client-Centered Therapy,* which provided some creative developments in theory, research, and practice as well as some expansions in application. Notable among these were a focus on the inner experience of the client as an essential focus of psychology and psychotherapy, including a theory of personality change presented by Eugene Gendlin that placed client processing of experiencing as an essential aspect of constructive change. Rogers developed a "process equation in therapy" that suggested that change in client-centered therapy had a number of threads: (a) a loosening in feelings from unexpressed to

freely expressed; (b) a change in the manner of experience from past recol-
lections to present experiencing of what is alive in the moment; (c) a shifting
of the "cognitive maps of experiencing" from rigid constructs of experience
to the creation of constructions of meaning that are more fluid and modifi-
able; (d) changes in the self toward increasing congruence between self and
experience; (e) increases in the effectiveness of client behavior, moving from
fear of relationships to freely living in relationships; and (f) increases in the
differentiation and clarity of feelings and meanings.

IV. A Period of Expansion in Practice (1970–1977)

In 1974, *Innovations in Client-Centered Therapy* was published by David
Wexler and Laura Rice. Other than a brief introductory statement on
the "Future of Client-Centered Therapy," Rogers did not write any other
chapters in this provocative text. This was not entirely surprising. While
Rogers was supportive of others in developing new ideas in the client-
centered framework, he may not have embraced all of those ideas. Instead,
Rogers typically relied on his own perceptions and experiences in the
creation of his theory and response styles but tended not to incorporate
ideas from others unless they fit his current or developing conceptualizations. As a consequence, some of the more creative ideas in *Innovations
in Client-Centered Therapy* made little impact on Rogers and, without
Rogers's endorsement or support, tended not to be integrated into the
fabric of client-centered thinking or application. Had he been supportive,
person-centered therapy may have evolved in other directions that would
likely have been accepted by many practitioners.

Despite Rogers's lack of support for the ideas presented in the *Innovations* book, many worthy and creative ideas were offered. Gendlin presented
a conceptualization of client-centered therapy that integrated experiential
focusing. Rice advocated for the use of what she termed the evocative
function of the therapist. In this modification of empathic responding,
the therapist intentionally used evocative reflections designed to heighten
the experiencing and processing of client emotion. These creative offerings
of Gendlin and Rice have been incorporated by many person-centered
therapists.

Innovations contained in the Wexler and Rice text included cognitive and information-processing views of client-centered therapy and the blending of gestalt and client-centered therapy. Other chapters addressed issues such as creativity and well-being, openness to experience in psychotherapy, encounter groups, and larger applications to social change. Except for Rice's and Gendlin's innovations, surprisingly few of these contributions have been integrated into the larger body of knowledge of client-centered therapy, though they remain fruitful sources for expanding the range and complexity of person-centered therapy.

V. Rogers's Last Years (1977–1987)

In 1977, Rogers published *Carl Rogers on Personal Power,* a text aimed at articulating the political and larger social impact associated with engaging in person-centered principles. Toward this end, it contained chapters on the politics of helping, on new views of what marriage and family might become, on concern for the powerless and oppressed, on educational trends, on intercultural tensions, and on the politics of administration and the emerging person. It was by far Rogers's greatest attempt to extend the reach and impact of his ideas.

Rogers's final 10 years were spent focused on reducing tensions between groups and countries at odds with each other and on effecting peace throughout the world. As Maureen O'Hara noted:

> In his last years, Rogers and various colleagues . . . took the client-centered message to over twenty countries, including: South Africa, where we facilitated encounters between blacks and whites; Latin America, where North encountered South; Europe, where Eastern bloc Marxists met Western humanists; and Ireland, where Protestants met Catholics. (Kirschenbaum, 2007, p. 495)

In 1980 Rogers published *A Way of Being,* which was a collection of previous articles and papers from the 1960s through the 1970s. In these essays, Rogers was intentionally and increasingly becoming more provocative as his own thinking progressed. His strongest positions include the humanization of educational methods with an emphasis on experiential learning. Clearly the influence of John Dewey is evident here. Another provocative paper was entitled "Do We Need 'a' Reality?" About this issue Rogers stated:

> The only reality I can possibly know is the world as *I* perceive it at this moment. The only reality *you* can possibly know is the world as you perceive and experience it at this moment. And the only certainty is that those perceived realities are different. There are as many "real worlds" as there are people. (1980, p. 102)

Because Rogers was primarily focused on larger applications during the last years of his life, he was little involved in developments in the theory or practice of psychotherapy. In 1986, when I was editor of the *Person-Centered Review*, I recall asking Rogers if he might want to revisit and revise his 1959 theory of personality and psychotherapy. In good humor he suggested that my encouraging suggestion made too much work for him and declined to revise any major aspect of his work. He did, however, develop further one key concept of his therapeutic work, that of therapist presence. Over 60 years of therapeutic practice had increasing convinced him that the quality of his presence, the manner in which he brought the core of his being to another person, was often full of healing. This point will be discussed further later.

In 1984, Ron Levant and John Shlien coedited *Client-Centered Therapy and the Person-Centered Approach*, which was a rich collection of ideas and applications. A number of the most compelling chapters will be summarized briefly in the following paragraphs. First, Neil Watson pointed out that Rogers's necessary and sufficient conditions hypothesis had never been fully tested because not all of Rogers's conditions, including measures of therapist-client contact and client incongruence, were included in the research designs. This criticism still holds today.

Germain Lietaer addressed the conundrum that, in client-centered theory, unconditional positive regard implied acceptance of the client's experience but not necessarily his or her concrete external behavior. Lietaer commented:

> Unconditionality refers to my acceptance of his experience. My client ought to experience the freedom to feel *anything* with me; he should

sense that I am open to his experience and will not judge it. . . . [However], this attitude of receptivity toward the inner experiential world of my client does not mean that I welcome all behavior equally. Both within and without the relationship there can be specific behaviors of which I disapprove, would like to change, or simply do not accept. (1984, pp. 46–47)

This clarification needed to be addressed since Rogers's concept of unconditional positive regard cannot possibly be manifested by all therapists for all clients' experiences, much less all behaviors, at all times. In contrast to Lietaer, Tom Gordon (1970) made an important distinction by indicating that persons could not be divorced from their behaviors (i.e., "I like you but not your behavior"). Rather, he understood that, at a given moment, we can only respond to the whole person and either find the behaving person acceptable or not in a given instance. Thus, unconditional positive regard for all persons in all situations was understood as an unattainable ideal rather than something therapists could actually offer without exception. What Gordon felt was most important was that the therapist's (or family member's) level of acceptance of another person was generally pervasive and unwavering. This view is consistent with my own experience. People/ clients do not expect that we will experience or display unconditional positive regard toward them no matter what they feel/experience or how they behave. What seems vital is that clients feel valued and that they will not be rejected or abandoned despite their therapists' dislike or disapproval of some of their attitudes, feelings, values, or behaviors. For therapists to act as if they were consistently unconditional in their regard would, at times, render them incongruent and therefore less trustworthy. That said, I believe it is also true that most person-centered therapists—especially the more mature, evolved, and grounded practitioners—have quite high levels of tolerance and acceptance that enable them to continue to feel compassion for and consistently value the vast majority of their clients, even those who are "hard to like" or have engaged in heinous behaviors.

In a chapter titled "Beyond Reflection: Emergent Forms of Empathy," Jerold Bozarth made the argument that empathy may take many forms and therefore is not limited to the most common empathic understanding responses. He made the provocative point that reflection itself is not empathy, though it may help the therapist communicate empathy. Bozarth posed the question, "How can the therapist experience the world of the client?" (1984, p. 69). His proposal was that therapists develop idiosyncratic modes of empathy based on the person of the therapist, the person of the client, and the manner of their interactions. He suggested that idiosyncratic empathy emphasizes: (a) the transparency of the therapist to the client, (b) the person-to-person encounter between therapist and client, and (c) the therapist's intuition. While Bozarth's position was provocative and not acceptable to all client-centered therapists, I believe it opened up more creative possibilities for entering and grasping the world of the client.

Eugene Gendlin realized that not all clients/people are oriented to or naturally skilled at focusing on inner experiences, but he learned that this skill is teachable. Subsequently, he developed more sophisticated and specific ways of enabling clients to contact and make therapeutic use of their felt sense. Because the client's felt sense is often vague, subtle, and elusive, the guidance of a skilled therapist is essential in helping the client maintain focus on the felt sense and discovering its implicit meaning.

Jules Seeman presented a compelling overview of theories of optimal functioning, including an expanded and fresh view and synthesis of what it means to be fully functioning. His major conclusions were that highly functioning persons are: (a) integrated and have positive self-concepts; (b) healthier, more in touch with their bodies and responsive to their feedback; (c) efficient in their perceptions of reality, able to generate more information and more differentiated information, experiencing more environmental contact and mastery; (d) able to function with greater intellectual efficiency that makes maximal use of their resources; (e) secure in their sense of self, confident, and trusting of themselves; (f) able to maintain a strong sense of self with a central organizing function that filters perception and the construction of reality, influences decisions and actions, and defines their sense of place in the world; (g) displaying a sense of autonomy that enhances both independent functioning and social relationships; and (h) in caring and generative relationships.

John Shlien offered a bold and provocative challenge of the psycho-analytic concept of transference. The first sentence of his seminal paper reads: "Transference is a fiction invented and maintained by the therapist to protect himself from the consequences of his own behavior" (1984, p. 153). He contends that the present-oriented client-centered therapy was less likely to evoke what seemed like transference in psychoanalytic therapy. Further, transparent client-centered therapists were not likely to elicit transference reactions since projection was less likely. In short, Shlien's position represents the views of most client-centered therapists who neither seek to elicit "transference" nor find it a useful concept in understanding therapist–client engagements. Shlien and most person-centered therapists take the position that seeming transference reactions are, in fact, manifestations of the client reacting to the therapist's manner of relating. Indeed, relational psychoanalysis, a contemporary version of psychoanalysis, takes the position that therapist and client constantly influence each other. Thus, relational psychotherapists eschew any belief in therapeutic neutrality and instead examine their contributions to their clients' reactions to them—a shift from a one-person to a two-person view of psychotherapy.

Barrett-Lennard articulated a person-centered systems view of family relationships while Bernard and Louise Guerney created psychoeducational models of therapy for children, couples, and families that drew heavily on person-centered theory.

One of the most prolific and substantive contributors to the develop-ment of person-centered theory and practice was Art Combs, a former student of Rogers at Ohio State University in the early 1940s. One of Combs's most valuable contributions was a summary of research evidence on perceptual/belief differences in good and bad helpers. Good help-ers: (a) were people oriented; (b) viewed clients from an internal frame of reference and attended to their personal meanings; (c) saw people as able; (d) were dependable, worthy, and friendly; (e) identified with others; (f) saw self as enough and confident in abilities; (g) saw self as revealing; and (h) saw their purposes as freeing the client, as altruistic in intent, and as concerned for larger meanings in life (Combs, 1986). These views resulted in therapists engaging in a cooperative partnership with their clients.

In 1986, Rogers responded to a question posed by the editor of the *Person-Centered Review* regarding what is most essential to the future development of the person-centered approach. Rogers commented in a manner that was consistent with his lifetime value regarding the importance of research as follows:

> There is only one way in which a person-centered approach can avoid becoming narrow, dogmatic and restrictive. That is through studies—simultaneously hardheaded and tender-minded—which open new vistas, bring new insights, challenge our hypotheses, enrich our theory, expand our knowledge, and involve us more deeply in an understanding of the phenomena of human change. (1986, p. 259)

Fortunately, a number of person-centered researchers were developing a variety of creative methods to address compelling questions. These approaches will be presented in the following sections.

VI. The Person-Centered Approach After Rogers (1987–present)

The founders of any therapeutic system exert an enormous, and often inordinate, influence on the way the therapy is conceived and practiced, often far beyond its inception. Freud (psychoanalysis), Adler (individual psychology), Perls (gestalt therapy), Ellis (rational emotive behavior therapy), and Rogers were creative and charismatic founders who drew many adherents to them who then extended outward the influence of their systems. Adherents tend to practice the therapy in a manner very similar to the founder and defend the originator's views as unshakeable truths to be preserved. Ironically, this is so despite the founders' often-stated expectation and hope that their model would continue to develop.

Rogers believed and hoped the person-centered approach would continue to evolve. In fact, he often expressed concern that client-centered therapy would become dogmatic and stifled in its development. Although Rogers' thinking did evolve, it is also true that the way he practiced therapy remained fairly constant until he died. Many client-centered therapists, especially the more traditional practitioners, continue to practice much as Rogers did or in even more conservative ways. However, Rogers was always receptive to and encouraging of innovative ideas that would advance theory and practice. In 1986, a year before his death, Rogers commented: " I hope . . . we're always on the move, to a new theory . . . to new areas of dealing with situations, new ways of being with persons. I hope that we're always a part of the 'growing edge'" (Cornelius-White & Cornelius-White, 2005, p. 396). Others, too, believed that client-centered therapy could be modified for the better and proposed newer ideas and varied forms of practice.

VARIETIES OF PERSON-CENTERED THERAPY

As will be noted in the forthcoming sections, many advances in the theory and practice were articulated during Rogers's lifetime. While Rogers encouraged such advances, he rarely supported them overtly, nor did he change his own theory or model of practice based on the alternatives proposed by others. The history of the development of various therapeutic models also shows that changes in the founder's model tend to occur slowly and gradually and take at least a few decades before being accepted as legitimate alternatives. This is the case with person-centered therapy. At this point, one can no longer say that there is only one form of person-centered therapy. Rather, myriad person-centered therapies now incorporate some of Rogers's basis premises while rejecting or modifying others. In 2000 Margaret Warner wrote a paper entitled "Person-Centered Psychotherapy: One Nation, Many Tribes," a designation that seems apropos. The major journal of person-centered therapy, founded in 2002 under the title *Person-Centered and Experiential Psychotherapies*, reflects the current reality that a variety of person-centered therapeutic approaches with diverse conceptualizations in theory and practice now exist. Many of the more recent versions have resulted in more creative and sophisticated styles of practice designed to be more effective with a broader range of clients and problems. If one thing is certain, it is that person-centered therapies will continue to evolve in future years as more is learned about how therapists and clients might engage more optimally with each other.

Classical Client-Centered Psychotherapy

The classical group of practitioners continues to uphold the position that the six core conditions articulated by Rogers in 1957 are both necessary and sufficient, that Rogers's 1959 theory of personality and psychotherapy remains definitive, and that nondirective attitude and behavior on the part of the therapist is essential to practice.

As Rogers developed his approach, he rarely used the term *nondirective* beyond the early 1950s and preferred instead to speak of creating conditions that "freed" the client. However, many in the classical and conservative branch of client-centered therapy believe that the truest form of client-centered therapy must be unwaveringly nondirective; in fact, they have described their approach as "nondirective client-centered therapy" (NDCCT). In a recent article, Grant (2004), one of nondirective therapy's strongest advocates, argued that absolute therapist nondirectiveness forms the ethical basis for the client's inalienable right to self-determination. This conservative group of client-centered therapists essentially views any deviance from complete nondirectiveness in behavior as some other form of therapy related to but not truly client-centered in spirit or practice. They view most innovations and variations from Rogers's model of the 1950s as something other than client-centered therapy. Some extreme members of this group have been scathing in their criticism and rejecting (i.e., "You are not one of us") toward those attempting to advance, supplement, or alter Rogers's earlier model. John Shlien was a member of this group, having been a student of Rogers and then a staff member and administrator at the University of Chicago Counseling Center until 1967. Shlien has expressed his preference "for 'pure forms' insofar as they can be developed" and a distaste for pragmatism, stating, "the kind of pragmatism that says 'whatever works' is not for me. Such pragmatists have no principles, only instruments, and by no means access to all available instruments either!" (2003, p. 218). Regarding persons who were developing new theory or innovative methods in practice, Shlien was skeptical and sometimes intolerant. He stated,

> What I hope is that they will do what they want to do, and call it what it is. It simply is not acceptable to pour old wine into new bottles, especially since it is the labels that are the sought after objects. (2003, pp. 218–219)

That some practitioners should maintain what appears to be a traditional and narrow view of client-centered therapy should not be surprising. There will always be practitioners of a specific approach who truly believe that the original position advanced by the founder will always remain its purest and best form. For some, the original or pure forms remain compelling while deviations feel like compromises and inaccuracies. The classical group continues to have a vocal and powerful voice in the person-centered community although its members probably represent a minority of person-centered therapists at this time. However, the down side of this position is often uncritical reverence for the founder and his ideas that results in a stifling of progress.

As Pete Sanders noted in a chapter on the history of client-centered therapy and the person-centered approach, "Client-Centered Therapy theory effectively stood still for over 20 years between the mid-sixties and the late eighties. He [Rogers] published brief, occasional essays related to therapy in this time, but none presented *new* theory" (2004, p.15).

I find Sanders's comments to be both accurate and telling. Except for defining therapist presence as a powerful way of being for the therapist, neither Rogers's theory nor manner of practice changed perceptibly in the last 30 years of his life. Despite many advances in theory and practice achieved by person-centered scholars and practitioners, Rogers himself was little affected by such innovations, though he did not oppose them. Nor did he endorse them, though he sometimes acknowledged them.

The next section presents an illustration of the classical version of person-centered psychotherapy, in the form of a case example of Rogers himself. The session was conducted in 1976 when Rogers was 74. Please note that the client's discussion of race in this session reflects the context of that time period. I have provided selective commentary as noted in the body of the transcript.

Therapeutic Illustration

This case of Rogers and Sylvia is taken from a chapter by David J. Cain (1996) in *The Psychotherapy of Carl Rogers*, edited by Farber, Brink, and Raskin. During the session Sylvia discloses, with great trepidation, her attraction to Black persons, about which she struggles with a myriad of conflicted feelings, including shame and uncertainty over whether her natural attraction may be pathological in some way or are understandable and acceptable. Sylvia is an attractive Caucasian woman who appears to be in her mid-30s and the mother of two children. Excerpts from her fifth session of a series of demonstration interviews with Rogers are presented.

Sylvia: There's something I've been wanting to talk over with you.

Rogers: OK.

Sylvia: It's, I'm real attracted to Black people. (C.R.: M-hm.) And, uh, that's about the craziest part of me, I'm ashamed. (C.R.: M-hm.) Um, I'm embarrassed, not right now this minute, but when I'm out walking around.

Rogers: When it happens, m-hm.

Sylvia: And living my life.

Rogers: You feel what an awful thing it is that "I'm attracted to Black people."

Sylvia: M-hm. Not all Black people I see but a lot. (C.R.: M-hm, m-hm.) And, like the Black people I talked it over with, it seems, it doesn't seem like any problem at all, they understand perfectly. (C.R.: M-hm, m-hm.) And, but my family, I think it's a real painful situation for them when I have as many Black friends as I do. (C.R.: M-hm, m-hm.) And—

Rogers: That sounds like not only your family looks down on it or something but that you scold yourself for it too.

Sylvia: Uh-huh. I, I think there's something wrong with me.

Rogers: Yeah, That's it.

Sylvia: M-hm. But it doesn't—

Rogers: What kind of crazy person am I that I feel attracted to so many Blacks?

Sylvia: I'm sick, sick, I think—

Rogers: Sick, that's—

Sylvia: And neurotic, um (C.R. Hmm) Strange. (C.R. Hmm)

Rogers: You really feel that there's something sick in you that causes you to have so many Black friends.

Commentary: Rogers both acknowledges and accepts Sylvia's puzzlement and felt disturbance over her attraction to Blacks as she tries to make sense of and come to terms with her experience. His empathic and accepting comments appear to help her wrestle with the conflicting reactions of her parents (representative of White culture) and the understanding attitudes she feels with her Black friends.

Sylvia: Well, I keep hoping for a reasonable explanation, and there is none.

Rogers: So there isn't any reason except that you feel this way.

Sylvia: M-hm. And I—

Rogers: And that isn't good enough.

Sylvia: Well, I, I, I've been struggling so long to accept that in myself, and I'm still fighting. It's like I'm fighting to accept that in myself and, and letting go rather than thinking it's a terrible thing and, and I can't let other people know. (C.R.: M-hm, m-hm, m-hm.) And, uh—

Rogers: It's that I should not feel that way. I shouldn't be that way. It's sick.

A few minutes later in the interview.

Sylvia: M-hm. And I tell myself I should be joyful, I mean (small laugh), why, why negative? (C.R.: M-hm, m-hm.) And I, I guess you know, the culture or I don't know, I— (sighs)

Rogers: But you feel disapproved of probably, certainly by your family and maybe by the culture in this respect.

Sylvia: My friends don't understand. (C.R.: M-hm, m-hm.). My White friends.

Rogers: M-hm. Makes you feel different. (Sylvia: M-hm) Set apart or something like that.

Commentary: Both Rogers and Sylvia identify her concern as having a strong cultural component. It is interesting to note that, while most cultural issues are experienced by minority clients, in this case Sylvia's own White cultural background has resulted in conflict for her.

Focusing-Oriented Psychotherapy

Focusing-oriented psychotherapy was developed by Eugene Gendlin, who is a philosopher, psychologist, and psychotherapist. While earning his Ph.D. in philosophy at the University of Chicago, he became a student of Rogers at the University of Chicago Counseling Center during the early 1950s. He joined the faculty of the University of Chicago in 1963 and taught there until 1995 when he retired.

Gendlin's original contribution is the concept of *experiencing*, which refers to "the process of concrete, bodily feelings, which constitute the basic matter of psychological and personality phenomena" (1970, p. 138) and to the awareness of an inwardly sensed, bodily felt event of an ongoing process. Gendlin views psychological disturbance as an impairment or block in the person's capacity for processing experience because, without this vital source of personal meaning, there is a constriction in living.

Gendlin now calls his approach focusing-oriented psychotherapy (1996). He fully acknowledges that his approach is grounded in a supportive relationship and client-centered listening. During the process of focusing-oriented therapy, the therapist helps the client become aware of and focus on the emerging bodily felt sense of the client's problem. Experiential focusing enables the client to draw on the wisdom of bodily knowing that creates a fresh understanding of a troublesome experience and points toward a more effective manner of living. In focusing-oriented psychotherapy, each felt sense is unique to the individual in the immediate moment and generates specific language to describe the experience. This contrasts with the way clients often describe their feeling states with words that are an imprecise approximation or general understanding rather than a specific moment's exact meaning.

The focusing process generally occurs in a number of definable steps. First, the client becomes aware of something at the edge of his or her consciousness. Initially this experiential awareness is vague, unclear, a bit illusive, and hard to grasp. The client senses something inside but doesn't yet know what it is or have words for it. As the client attends to the felt sense, awareness of the bodily, somatic sensation of the problem emerges clearly enough to be contacted and referred to. This sensation is experienced as an intricate whole. As the client attends to this bodily felt sense, words or images (sometimes sounds or gestures) may come that exactly express the implicit message or meaning. For example, the client might describe the felt sense as a "feeling of dread about dealing with a difficult person." As the client attends further, the felt sense unfolds and becomes clearer, and a "shift" or step occurs in which the felt sense changes subtly and another level of understanding occurs. For example, the client becomes clear that the dread is about being criticized or belittled by her boss. As the therapist and client attend together to the emerging felt sense, further shifts in the bodily sense continue and new meanings become clear. These shifts come with a sense of "rightness" and relief since what was once fuzzy and murky is now clear. The client often experiences something like "Oh, that's what it is!" This distinct sense of movement is bodily and is called a "felt shift" or "carrying forward." Even though what is now clearly understood may be unpleasant, there is a sense of relief and calmness that one knows the meaning of the felt sense. Often there are a series of shifts and steps forward as the client moves from one understanding to a fresh variation. These steps tend to lead to a sense of freshness and personal insight that becomes more refined as the client continues to reflect on its meaning and implications for more effective living.

A client of mine, upon reporting what she experienced as she completed a session of experiential focusing commented that she felt "fresh" and "new." Many clients report similar experiences, including a feeling of confidence in the "ring of truth" that typically occurs as the felt sense unfolds and clarifies. It is not unusual for clients to experience some surprise over what is discovered, partly because their initial cognitive explanation of the felt sense turns out to be something other than what was imagined initially. The focusing process itself is often experienced as "freeing," as what was once a mysterious unknown has transformed into a sense of clarity. The process of focusing seems to have its own therapeutic value as clients become better attuned to themselves, learn to live well in the moment, feel pride and confidence in their developing capacity for inner knowing, and trust their ability to make grounded decisions. Over time clients learn to focus on their own and tend to pay more attention to the unclear stirrings they experience in everyday life, thus becoming their own therapists.

Gendlin's focusing-oriented therapy, and especially the process of experiential focusing, have been incorporated into the practice of various forms of person-centered therapy, often in a seamless manner. The next section presents a case example of focusing-oriented psychotherapy.

Therapeutic Illustration

The client is a woman in her 70s who is facing difficult health issues. I have selected an interaction that shows what focusing-oriented therapy looks like when it is going well. Both client and therapist know how to attend to the felt sense and welcome the small steps of movement that come. The characteristic markers of effective experiential focusing include the use of the present tense, groping to find words for what is felt but not yet explicit, quiet and reflective pauses, and the emergence of metaphor, all visible in this transcript. Each statement has been annotated so the reader can see the change process.

C: I feel some way that I am not used to. (This is a felt sense. She is directly sensing some way she feels that is new to her—she does not yet have words for it. She does not know what it is.)

T: Uummm . . . so some way of feeling that you are not used to. (The therapist is comfortable with the "not yet knowing." He does not try to define this "some way" but invites her to sense into it.)

C: Something is different about my thinking—the ideas don't flow like they used to . . . (silent as she senses more into the "something"). It has to do with aging and poor health. (The phrase "has to do with" indicates that the "something" is not yet clear, but she can sense the "area" it is in.)

T: So it has to do with aging and poor health. (Again the therapist stays right with the unclearness while acknowledging the little bit of content that has come.)

C: It's like . . . I'm a patchwork quilt . . . I'm made up of so many different pieces all stitched together . . . but now it feels like I'm coming apart at the seams (begins to cry). I'm thinned. The quilt needs repair, it needs to be stitched back together, but then it is not strong where it's been stitched back, it's thinned. That's like the surgeries. They keep cutting open my body and stitching it back together. (This is the creative moment in which a metaphor emerges—the quilt—and a word, "thinned," that captures her felt sense exactly. Her tears are expressing both the pain of her illness and treatment and the relief of the inner movement, the carrying forward of her experiencing.)

T: There is a thinning in the quilt which is you. (The therapist just gently welcomes what has come. He does not ask further questions. He knows that her metaphor is exact and needs no addition or changing by him. This is one whole round of focusing. Now her body is clear for whatever next thing will arise.)

Although experiential focusing tends to be a process engaged in primarily by person-centered and humanistic therapists, sensitivity to these processes helps make any orientation more effective. Consequently, experiential focusing has been incorporated into many therapeutic approaches.

Emotion-Focused (Process-Experiential) Psychotherapy

Others followed Gendlin's lead and developed a variety of means to assist the client in processing emotional, bodily felt experiences to illuminate their meanings and implications for growth and change. Laura N. Rice (1974) extended the client-centered response style by developing the method of *evocative reflection*, which she viewed as a more active, vivid, and powerful form of client-centered empathy. The aim of evocative reflections is to "open up the experience and provide the client with a process whereby he can form successively more accurate constructions of his own experience"

(p. 290). The goal is to enable the client to reprocess experience in an undistorted manner that results in the reorganization of old and dysfunctional schemes. Rice believes that "if the client can fully explore his reactions to one such situation, and become aware of the elements in a more accurate and balanced form . . . the effect will be to force reorganization of all of the relevant schemes" (p. 294).

Working originally with Rice, Leslie Greenberg and colleagues Robert Elliott, Jeanne Watson, and Rhonda Goldman have blended the essence of client-centered therapy with elements of gestalt therapy, existentialism, and Rice's and Gendlin's experiential methods, into an empirically supported therapy they have called *emotion-focused therapy* (EFT), sometimes referred to as *process-experiential therapy.*

Pos and Greenberg describe EFT as

> An empirically supported humanistic treatment that views emotions as centrally important in the experience of self, in both adaptive and maladaptive functioning, and in therapeutic change. EFT involves a style that combines both following and guiding the client's experiential process, and emphasizes the importance of both relationship and intervention skills. It takes emotion as the fundamental datum of human experience while recognizing the importance of meaning making, and ultimately views emotion and cognition as inextricably intertwined. (2006, p. 1)

In EFT, emotions are viewed as having an inherently adaptive potential that, if activated, attended to, and processed, enable clients to alter problematic emotional states and troublesome self-experiences. The emotion theory on which EFT is based suggests that client emotion influences modes of processing, guides attention, and enhances memory. A considerable amount of client behavior is seen as oriented toward emotion regulation and attachment. People do not only do things because of their view of things but because it feels good or bad. Emotions are understood as expressions of clients' most essential needs, signals that alert them to the state of their well-being and as guides to take action in meeting essential needs. From an emotion-focused perspective, disorder is seen as resulting from failures in the regulation of affect, avoidance of affect, traumatic learning, and lack of processing of emotion (Elliott, Watson, Goldman, & Greenberg, 2004).

Grounded in a client-centered relationship, Greenberg is clear in emphasizing that the client and the quality of the relationship always take precedence over the therapeutic tasks proposed, methods, or goals. All tasks are mediated through the empathic bond that is formed out of careful following and empathic attunement. The EFT therapist also realizes that task collaboration is paramount and that productive therapy cannot occur unless the client and therapist are working together to solve the client's problems.

The EFT therapist follows the flow of the client's internal experience as it evolves from moment to moment and remains empathically attuned to and communicates back the client's immediate inner experience for further processing. Process guidance is also provided to the client by the EFT therapist who serves as an experiential guide or coach who is knowledgeable about the subjective terrain and emotional processes.

Three phases of EFT are identified (Greenberg, 2002; Pos & Greenberg, 2006):

Phase I: Bonding and Awareness. In the initial stage, the therapist engages an empathic attitude and positive regard to create a safe environment for evoking and exploring emotion. The client is also provided a rationale for how working with emotions is likely to be helpful. In this stage a focus for therapy that addresses the client's main concerns is established.

Phase II: Evocation and Exploration. In this phase emotions are evoked and explored with a goal of identifying the client's deepest level of primary emotion. EFT therapists may employ a number of methods in this process, including evocative empathy, experiential focusing, and gestalt chair dialogues. Clients are also assisted, as needed, to deal with any problems they may experience in working with their emotions.

Phase III: Transformation and Generation of Alternatives. As the client works with a core emotion, the emphasis shifts to the construction of more effective ways of responding emotionally, cognitively, and behaviorally. Specifically, the client learns ways to access more adaptive emotional responses and create new meanings and self-narratives that result in a more resilient and integrated sense of self.

Therapeutic Illustration

The following excerpt is taken from the case of Lisa, a 27-year-old Caucasian woman who was married and had two young children. She was struggling with depression and sought therapy for help to deal with her husband's gambling problem and to achieve greater self-understanding. She received 15 sessions of emotion-focused therapy. In session 8, presented here, the client is engaged in an empty-chair dialogue where she enacts her imaginary husband in the other chair:

C: Yeah, be quiet, just shut up, you know, don't tell anybody. It's our problem (referring to his gambling).

T: Keep it in the family.

C: Yeah, just keep it between you and I, and you don't have to go around telling people our problems. You and I can solve this, or we can take care of it ourselves—nobody needs to know.

She continues, repeating phrases she has heard from her husband that weaken and invalidate her, such as "this is just the way I am," "I can handle my own problems," "I'm much better than I was before," and "I enjoy doing what I do, and I like it." In response to her husband in the other chair, she finds her own voice and begins to assert herself.

C: Yeah, I deserve a lot better than what you've given me. Just putting me aside. It's like leaving a dog at home all the time and never letting him out.

T. Uh-huh. You feel very trapped.

C: Yeah, I'm tired of feeling trapped and isolated and believing that this is the way marriage is, but no! This is not the way and I don't want it.

T: Uh huh.

C: I'm really tired of it.

T: I'm tired of it.

C: Really tired of it. I'm tired of covering and being phony and just pretending everything's okay but it's not and that makes me angry now when I try to protect, that it's okay when it's not.

In this dialogue, we see how the client accesses pride and angry self-assertion in relation to a husband by whom she has felt oppressed and unable to stand up for herself. For her this is a shift in emotional processing.

Pre-Therapy

A version of person-centered therapy called pre-therapy has shown promise in helping severely impaired persons. Pre-therapy was created by Garry Prouty and colleagues (Prouty, 1994; Prouty, VanWerde, & Portner, 2002) because "normative therapy procedures generally do not work effectively with this population for two reasons: (a) People with psychoses have far more difficulty in forming interpersonal connections and relationships; (b) people with psychoses have far more difficulty in interpersonal communication than do those without psychoses" (Cain & Seeman, 2002, p. 590). Traditional person-centered empathic understanding responses needed to be modified because they were simply not sufficient in making contact with chronic schizophrenic, psychotic, and mentally retarded persons and other low-functioning clients such as those with autism and dementia.

Psychological Contact

Prouty recognized that making "psychological contact" with such severely *contact-impaired* persons was an enormous challenge that required substantial modifications in practice. Prouty defines *psychological contact* as the "lived, pre-reflective conscious experience of the world, self or other" (Cain & Seeman, 2002, p. 591). The term *Pre-therapy* was used to emphasize that psychological contact is a *precondition* for therapy for persons with whom it is difficult to make meaningful contact (e.g., an hallucinating person). Pre-therapy is a creative extension of person-centered and experiential therapies, influenced by Rogers, Gendlin, and Perls. Rogers himself acknowledged the historical importance of Prouty's work as well as its innovative nature.

Psychological contact with clients is achieved through three primary means: (1) contact reflections, (2) contact functions, and (3) contact behaviors.

Contact Reflections. At the heart of pre-therapy are what Prouty refers to as *contact reflections,* defined as "duplicative, literal and concrete responses to the client's limited level of expression" (Cain & Seeman, 2002, p. 591). There are five varieties of contact reflections:

1. *Situational reflections* (SR) communicate the concrete reality of the client's situation, environment, or milieu. An example is "You are sitting in the corner."
2. *Facial reflections* (FR) communicate the client's pre-expressive feelings and facilitate affective contact between client and therapist. An example is: "You look angry."
3. *Word-for word reflections* (WWR) communicate exactly what the client has just said when the client's language is disorganized or difficult to comprehend (e.g., echolalia, word salad, neologisms). For example, the client says, "dog, tree" and the therapist responds with "dog, tree." The intent is to restore comprehensible communication in the client.
4. *Body reflections* (BR) communicate the client's bizarre body expression such as catatonia or echopraxia (involuntary repeating of another's body expression). A body reflection may be (a) a verbal reflection (e.g., "You are waving your arm") or (b) a literal reflection or imitation of the client's body expression (e.g., assuming the posture of the client).
5. *Reiterative reflections* (RR) attempt to re-contact the client. When any kind of contact reflection succeeds in eliciting a response from the client, it is repeated in an attempt to strengthen the communication between client and therapist.

Therapeutic Illustration

Prouty (1994) describes the application of contact reflections in resolving a psychotic episode with a woman diagnosed as schizophrenic. A mental health paraprofessional (referred to as "the therapist" in the example) took a group of seven halfway house residents, including the woman with schizophrenia, on a community visit. She was seated in the rear seat of the van. The therapist comments: "As I looked in the rear-view mirror, I observed the client crouched down into the seat with one arm outstretched over her head. Her face was filled with terror, and her voice began to escalate in screams. I pulled the van off the road and asked the volunteer to take the other patients out of the van. I sat next to the client, sharing the seat. The client's eyes were closed, and she was wincing with fear."

Client: (In a rising voice) It's pulling me in.

Therapist (WWR): It's pulling me in.

(Client continues to slip further down into the seat, with her left arm outstretched, eyes still closed.)

Therapist (BR): Your body is slipping down into the seat. Your arm is in the air.

Therapist (SR): We are in the van. You are sitting next to me.

(This exchange is repeated a few times.)

Therapist (FR): Something is frightening you. You are screaming.

Client: (screaming) It's sucking me in!

Therapist (WWR): It's sucking you in.

Therapist (SR/BR): We are in the van, Carol. You are sitting next to me. Your arm is in the air.

Client: (beginning to sob very hard, arms dropped to lap) It was the vacuum cleaner.

Therapist (WWR): It was the vacuum cleaner.

Client: (making direct eye contact) She did it with the vacuum cleaner. (Continuing in a normal tone of voice) I thought it was gone. She used to turn on the vacuum cleaner when I was bad and put the hose right on my arm. I thought it sucked it in (Less sobbing. It should be noted that daily, this patient would kiss her arm up to her elbow and stroke it continually).

Therapist (BR): Your arm is still here. It didn't get into the vacuum cleaner.

(Client smiled and was held by the therapist.)

Later that afternoon, a professional psychotherapy session was held, and the client began to delve into her feelings about punishment received as a child. It should be noted that medications were not needed to resolve the crisis.

Contact Functions. Contact functions are designed to increase the client's awareness of and connection to the world, the self, and others. These "ego functions" are intended to develop or restore reality, affective and communicative contact necessary for therapy to take place. Contact functions include reality contact (awareness of people, places, things, and events), affective contact (awareness of moods, feelings, and emotions), and communicative contact (symbolization of one's reality and affect to others). Contact functions are basic types of awareness and abilities in most people but need to be developed and cultivated in people who are severely impaired. A primary role of the therapist is to help to facilitate development of these functions.

Contact Behaviors. Contact behaviors represent clients' emerging behaviors that result from the facilitation of contact functions through therapist contact reflection. They are tangible and measurable behaviors communicated through either words or emotional expression and include the client's verbalization of tangible reality (persons, places, things, and events) and expression of affects (moods, feelings, and emotions).

Pre-therapy is a powerful means to enable clients to make meaningful contact and engage effectively with the therapist. Therapists incorporating pre-therapy processes have been able to engage with people who previously seemed unreachable. Not only do therapists realize that "there is someone in there" but that person is more sentient than previously believed, can be understood, and has something meaningful to say. In sum, pre-therapy constitutes a creative and needed approach to working with a variety of severely impaired persons.

Person-Centered Expressive Arts Psychotherapy

Carl Rogers's daughter, Natalie Rogers, has developed an approach to psychotherapy that integrates the use of creative expressive modes with person-centered principles. Thus, Natalie Rogers embraces her father's basic philosophy that "Each individual has worth, dignity and the capacity for self-direction if given an empathic, non-judgmental, supportive environment" (Rogers, n.d.). She also credits other prominent humanistic psychologists who have influenced the development of person-centered expressive arts therapy, including Abe Maslow, Rollo May, Clark Moustakas, Art Combs, and Sidney Jourard. What these pioneers share, according to Natalie Rogers, is a relational model of personal growth in which the therapist respects the client's dignity, value, and capacity for self-direction.

A foundational premise of Natalie Rogers's approach is that the therapeutic process "helps awaken creative life-force energy [and] what is creative is frequently therapeutic" (in Cooper, O'Hara, Schmid, & Wyatt, 2007, p. 316). Among the modalities employed are dance, music, and art therapies; journaling; poetry; imagery; meditation; improvisational drama; and any other means of creative expression that clients might wish to use. Natalie Rogers has observed that the use of one expressive art form often fosters the use of others, resulting in a "creative connection" that enhances the process of self-discovery while deepening affective experiences and finding personal meaning. Art is understood as a form of language that provides an "alternative path for intuitive, imaginative abilities supplementing traditional, logical, linear thought [that] . . . move the client into emotions yet add a further dimension, release of the 'free-spirit'" (in Cooper et al., 2007, p. 318). According to Rogers, clients indicate that the use of creative arts enables them to discover and deepen their sense of self, identify inner truths and values, transcend problems, achieve a fresh sense of their soul or spirit, and bring about constructive change.

During therapy, at moments when the client is experiencing a strong emotion, the therapist offers an option to express the emotion though creative means. The client may accept or refuse the invitation and the therapist honors the client's preference. When clients choose to use creative means, the therapist serves as an empathic but silent witness until the process is completed. At that point the therapist might inquire about the client's experience during the process of creative expression. The client and therapist view the creation together while the therapist encourages the client to begin to identify personal meaning in the expression. The therapist remains non-interpretative, though he or she may encourage further exploration or offer ideas about the possible meanings of the client's expression. Similar to person-centered therapy, the therapist checks to see if he or she accurately understands the meanings inherent in the client's creations.

Natalie Rogers indicates that person-centered expressive therapies have been found helpful with a number of populations and problems including self-help groups, 12-step substance abuse programs, persons who have been sexually abused, grieving persons, anger problems, and children in play therapy. A research study conducted on 32 participants of Rogers's workshops found increases in self-awareness, improved self-confidence, and deeper self-exploration (Merrill & Anderson, 1993).

In sum, Natalie Rogers's expressive arts therapy represents a major innovation in practice and helped open the way for other person-centered therapists to expand the variety and range of practice.

Existential Influences on Person-Centered Psychotherapy

Existential philosophy and psychotherapy in various forms have influenced the thinking of client-centered therapists for several decades, beginning with Carl Rogers. Rogers had dialogues with existential philosophers Martin Buber in 1957 and with Paul Tillich in 1965. Over many years, Rogers corresponded and dialogued in person with Rollo May and had some contact with R. D. Laing. He was also appreciative of the ideas of existential philosopher Soren Kierkegaard. Regarding the relationship of existential thought to client-centered therapy, Rogers (1980) wrote, "I felt greatly supported in my new approach, which I found to my surprise was a home-grown brand of existential philosophy" (p. 39). Both person-centered therapy and existential philosophy are fundamentally grounded in Husserl's phenomenological view, which takes the position that human beings need to be understood in terms of their tangible, lived experience. Relatedly, existential philosophers emphasized the uniqueness of each person, a position that contrasts with a positivistic scientific worldview that tends to define persons in terms of their general or average characteristics. Both Rogers and existentialists view the person as a process, a moving and changing being, as opposed to a static entity that can be categorized.

Mick Cooper (2004) summarizes what he sees as the similarities of existential and client-centered views. He suggests that both approaches tend to (a) emphasize the uniqueness and individuality of each client and of each therapeutic encounter; (b) understand clients in terms of their "subjective," lived experiences, rather than from an external, diagnostic perspective; (c) see psychological problems as a result of the distortion or denial of experiences and assert that an acknowledgement of one's true being can lead to a greater intensity and fullness of living; (d) reject or de-emphasize the use of techniques in therapy, emphasizing instead the importance of a genuine, spontaneous, human encounter; and (e) emphasize the importance of accepting and validating clients, however bizarre or maladaptive their behavior might seem. To these points I would add that both positions trust the client's capacity or potential to make positive and constructive choices. They also embrace such concepts as freedom, choice, autonomy, personal responsibility, and finding meaning in life.

There are also concepts in existential therapeutic approaches that may serve to heighten person-centered therapists' awareness of fundamental life issues with which all persons must grapple. In *Existential Psychotherapy* (1980), a text that is considered by many to be the most comprehensive, in-depth explication of the existential approach to psychotherapy, Irvin Yalom identified four of these issues, which he termed ultimate concerns: (a) death, (b) freedom, (c) isolation, and (d) meaninglessness. Other issues identified by existential therapists include "thrownness" (forces or events beyond one's control), capacity for awareness, anxiety as an inevitable aspect of the human condition, and the fact that we are essentially embodied. While the client in person-centered therapy determines the direction and focus of therapy, a greater sensitivity to such existential issues and challenges will enable the person-centered therapist to recognize and respond with greater understanding and depth when these issues arise.

Existential therapists tend to engage various aspects of themselves in an attempt to engage their clients with fundamental life issues. They are generally more active in style and more willing and inclined to confront clients with their self-deceptions and avoidance of critical aspects of their lives and the consequences of how they choose to live. Their manner of encounter is often more challenging and proactive in relationship to their clients than their person-centered counterparts, though their intent is in the service of awareness and growth. In an analysis of the differences and similarities of existential and classical client-centered therapists, Cooper concludes that "despite the divergences in philosophical and psychological opinion, both approaches are fundamentally committed to understanding human beings in the most dignified, respectful and validating way possible" (2003, p. 54).

INTEGRATIVE APPROACHES TO PERSON-CENTERED THERAPY

Integrative person-centered therapists subscribe to most aspects of Rogers's therapeutic system but also blend or integrate with it their own life experiences and ideas or those from other compatible therapeutic approaches (e.g., existential, gestalt, experiential) into a cohesive whole. Worsley (2004) suggests that

> Responsible integration within the Person-Centered Approach aims at an imaginative use of various theories and philosophies of therapy to stimulate an increased openness to experience within the therapist . . . [and] to link back the process of integration to the basic philosophy so as to demonstrate coherence. (p. 126)

Worsley goes on to suggest that integration implies an openness and receptivity to: (a) new conceptions of person-centered theory, (b) theory and insights from other models of therapy, (c) concepts generated from humanistic and other psychological theories, (d) philosophical knowledge that might inform therapy, and (e) various therapeutic practices that can be compatibly integrated.

Integrative models of person-centered therapy arose, in part, because some practitioners found the classical approach too constraining or lacking effectiveness in various ways. In terms of practice, an integrative approach suggests that person-centered therapy is implemented in a manner compatible with each therapist's personal convictions and personal style. I suspect a substantial portion of person-centered practitioners are, in fact, integrative, as relatively few adhere to a strictly classical client-centered model. Variations occur, for some, in how the core conditions are implemented. For others, bringing their own perspectives to the client for consideration or engaging various aspects of the self of the therapist are viewed as integrative. Conversely, some concepts and therapeutic methods are generally seen as incompatible (e.g., behavioral) though such approaches may be negotiated with the client for brief periods. In Worsley's view, whatever is incorporated "needs to be filtered through the fundamental philosophical stance of the person-centered approach" (2004, p. 139). Without such integration with the fundamental person-centered philosophy, the approach would be essentially eclectic, which would be more diverse in practice but lack cohesiveness.

Others who consider themselves integrative person-centered therapists tend to hold some of Rogers's beliefs as essential while viewing others as of lesser importance, questionable, possibly unnecessary, or even wrong. Some integrative therapists experience ambivalence or discontent with classical practitioners and regard the requirement for absolute nondirectiveness in attitude and behavior as questionable and limiting. Regarding this issue, Merry states:

> I aim to bring my whole self to my client as best I can. Sometimes it feels risky . . . but to confine the self is untherapeutic; I want to bring as much as possible of who I am, how I think and learn and feel, to my relationship with the client. . . . (Worsley, 2004, p. 132)

It is of critical importance that therapists' integration enables them to feel grounded and congruent in what they believe, feel, and do. Thus, integrative person-centered therapy has its own challenges. Not only must the therapist do more thinking and experimentation, but the therapist also must be clear about who he or she is and how that self can best be engaged with the client in a conceptually cohesive manner.

CONTEMPORARY DEVELOPMENTS IN PERSON-CENTERED PSYCHOTHERAPY

Person-centered theory and practice continue to evolve, something Rogers always expected and hoped for. In 1986, within a year before his death, Rogers gave a speech at the University of Chicago during a "Beyond Words

Symposium." During his speech Rogers reminisced about the history of the client/person-centered movement. At the end of the speech Rogers offered some thoughts about the future:

> . . . it's part of the whole pushing forward that I feel is part of the client-centered ethos that we don't stay in one spot. I hope. I hope we're always on the move, to a new theory, new ways of being, to new areas of dealing with situations, new ways of being with persons. I hope we're always a part of the "growing-edge." (Cornelius-White & Cornelius-White, 2005, p. 396)

Clearly Rogers was hopeful that his theory and its manner of implementation would break *new* ground and continue to progress. I suspect he would be pleased that variations of his model have evolved. In the few decades since Rogers's passing, there have been a number of advances in the ways person-centered psychotherapy might be conceptualized and practiced. In the next sections, I will review some of the most substantial advances, many of which have emanated from Europe.

BROADENING THE SCOPE OF THEORY AND PRACTICE

Although there has been understandable and expected resistance to expanding the scope of the therapist's repertoire of responses and therapeutic methods, such alterations are inevitable and necessary if person-centered therapy is to become more effective with clients who do not respond well to the classical approach and with clients experiencing more severe and intractable forms of psychopathology. As in all therapeutic approaches, many practitioners modify and supplement their style of practice to meet the needs of challenging clients. In the person-centered community, a number of practitioners have advocated the incorporation of a variety of methods. One of the first to advocate for the "supplementation" of person-centered therapy was Reinhard Tausch, who is one of the most productive and respected researchers and practitioners in person-centered therapy and education. Aware that Tausch and his colleagues were incorporating methods drawn from other approaches (e.g., systematic desensitization) into the person-centered model of therapy, Rogers visited Tausch's clinic in Germany and encouraged his broadened approach (Kirschenbaum, 2007). During a workshop in 1975 Rogers commented, "One thing about the client-centered approach is that I think it can utilize many modes from other points of view and yet keep a basically person-centered philosophy" (in Francis, 2009, p. 16).

In the late 1980s, Tausch's research on the effectiveness of person-centered therapy led him to conclude that,

> We as client-centered psychotherapists help some of our clients only insufficiently . . . it became clear to me [through research studies] that client-centered psychotherapy was a valuable experience in which many people changed significantly. However, some of the clients experienced little or no lasting changes toward greater emotional health. (Lietaer, Rombauts, & Van Balen, 1990, p. 447)

Tausch recognized a dilemma faced by all models of therapy, namely that there are inevitable limits to the effectiveness with some clients no matter how faithfully and competently the model is implemented by the therapist. Such clients are ultimately instructive because they cause us to constantly reevaluate the effectiveness of what we do and make needed modifications in practice. Tausch was also aware that "clients are occasionally looking for a stimulating facilitation of their self-explorative, cognitive restructuring, information about possibilities of alternative behaviors [and that] . . . many experience this as a very helpful support" (Lietaer, Rombauts, & Van Balen, 1990, p. 448). He recognized that if therapists were receptive, they would draw from the body of existing information in the fields of psychology, psychiatry, and various schools of psychotherapy on behalf of their clients' well-being. In other words, the needs of a given client supersede the therapist's allegiance to a theory and its typical manner of implementation. This is as it should be if we view helping clients grow and deal with their concerns as our primary commitment.

Tausch offered some useful criteria for choosing specific supplements to person-centered therapy. He posed the questions: "What is helpful for *this* client?" and "What does *he* need to facilitate his emotional health?" Thus, Tausch is pragmatically client-centered in searching for whatever might be effective. This was Rogers's initial approach when he was beginning to develop his ideas in Rochester. As the reader will recall, Rogers's guiding question was "Does it work?" Compatible with person-centered values, Tausch suggested that the therapist should not be directive in offering alternatives but, rather, respectful of the client's phenomenal world and desires, thus supporting the client's locus of evaluation. Tausch was clear that any possibilities offered to the client for consideration must be validated by empirical research. He also proposed that any supplements offered should not be a barrier to client-centered communication. Another criterion was that such supplementations facilitate the client's independence from the therapist and have a positive effect on the client's self-efficacy during and after therapy.

Tausch proposed some specific supplementations, including (a) relaxation techniques; (b) fear- and stress-reducing techniques; (c) behavior therapy techniques (e.g., time management, skills training, self-control methods); and (d) medical treatment of biochemical disturbances. Tausch's suggested supplements are obviously not exhaustive. Their main value is alerting the therapist to what else the therapist might do on behalf of the client who may not find traditional client-centered therapy to be sufficient in dealing with specific problems.

One of the more important implications of Tausch's proposal is that it broadens the definition of "client-centered" to include offering "additional therapeutic possibilities which are suited to the individual client's needs [including] . . . all the scientifically validated options which can help the individual client change his cognitions, emotional-physical reactions and behavior" (Lietaer, Rombauts, & Van Balen, 1990, pp. 453–454). This shift is of enormous import because it recognizes that the core conditions are *not sufficient* for some clients and provides clients viable options that are effective. Further, the therapist is freed to bring to the client any and all resources that may be of assistance to the client. Many other person-centered scholars and practitioners (e.g., Mearns & Cooper, 2005; Watson, Goldman, & Warner, 2002) have offered similar suggestions for integration of concepts and methods from other schools of thought with person-centered therapy.

On this topic, Art Combs, one of the primary developers of person-centered theory and practice, has noted that the therapist's fundamental resource is his or her self. In using one's self, Combs suggests, "Professional helpers must be creative persons able to select or invent appropriate responses on the spot" (1989, p. 96).

RELATIONAL DEPTH

One of the major changes in person-centered therapy is the therapist's increasing use of self in more diverse, intimate, and creative ways. While Rogers embraced this direction as he became aware of how impactful his focused presence was on the client, others have developed further how the person of the therapist may be used constructively on the client's behalf. David Mearns and Mick Cooper, coauthors of *Working at Relational Depth in Counseling and Psychotherapy* (2005) make a powerful case for the level and quality of contact between therapist and client. They define relational depth as a "state of profound contact and engagement between two people, in which each person is fully real with the Other, and able to understand and value the Other's experiences at a high level" (p. xii). Relational depth refers to moments of intense and intimate encounter as well as an enduring quality of contact and interconnection between two persons. Therapists working at relational depth have a high level of presence and are immersed in, accessible to, and responsive to their clients. They are sensitively attuned and resonate intuitively to all aspects of their client's communication, behavior, and being. They are receptive to being affected and influenced by their clients as they experience a sense of "weness" in their contact. Quite naturally, the therapist appreciates and affirms the client as a person of value. Relational depth also involves a dialogical relationship in which there is more mutuality of engagement and spontaneous expression by therapist and client than there is in the typically more one-sided relationship of the classical client-centered approach where therapists share relatively little of themselves as they focus primarily on entering their clients' worlds.

Person-centered therapists such as Mearns, Thorne, Cooper, and Schmid, along with humanistic, existential, gestalt, and relational psychoanalysts and feminist therapists, are leading the way in reconceptualizing the therapeutic endeavor. In this evolving model, therapist and client are partners in cocreating a relationship that is dialogic, egalitarian, and bidirectional in influence and that views the quality of the relationship as a source of experiential learning that enables clients to relate to the therapist, themselves, and others in a more present, intimate, disclosing, rich, satisfying, and healthy manner. Judith Jordan captures the sense of "mutual intersubjectivity" that characterizes relational therapies as she points to how the therapist and client are

> . . . both affecting the other and being affected by the other; one extends oneself out to the other and is also receptive to the impact of the other. There is openness to influence, emotional availability, and a constant changing pattern of responding to and affecting the other's state. There is both receptivity and active initiative toward the other. (1991, p. 82)

In essence, clients learn to be more effective social beings by participating in a mutual and vibrant meeting with their therapists. By so doing, clients experience themselves in different ways that result in the alteration of their self-concepts and quality of relationships with others.

A major shift in the theory of how the person is conceived is at the heart of how a more "relational" person-centered therapy might be understood and practiced. In Rogers's theory, the person is understood in primarily individualistic terms, viewed as a discrete and autonomous being. Since this view holds for therapist and client, person-centered therapy is conceived as a meeting between two separate persons.

An alternative and increasingly emerging view is that persons exist primarily in relationship to each other, rather than as separate entities. In this view, many contemporary philosophers and psychologists take the position that we are inextricably intertwined with each other and that we are best understood as "beings-in-relationship" (e.g., Friedman, 1985; Mearns & Cooper, 2005) From birth on, we exist first with others and only in relationships do we become ourselves and know ourselves. As infants, we can only know and define ourselves in interaction with our significant others. As Harry Stack Sullivan (1947) argued, we form our identities through the reflected appraisals of our parents and significant others. Throughout the life cycle we continue to alter our self-concepts based on the way we see ourselves through others' eyes. Further, in our daily lives much of what we think, feel, or do has reference to others, even though we may not think in these terms in the moment. We often have fantasies about others or "mental conversations" with people who are not present or are deceased. Much of our lives are spent in a wide variety of interactions with others—family, friends, teachers, coworkers, salespersons, people in novels, professional athletes, and so forth. As Cooper and Mearns note, "at the level of lived-being, we are constantly interacting with others, or thinking about others, or imagining doing things with others " (2005, p. 5). In short, most of our lives are related, in one way or another, to other people. Further, in many cultures the "self" is viewed not as an separate entity but rather as interdependent, interconnected, in relationship to others, as part of a larger whole that includes the physical world.

The case can be made that both positions, individualistic versus beings-in-relationship, are useful lenses through which we might conceive of ourselves. Subjectively, we often feel ourselves to be separate and independent entities when we are alone or even in the presence of others. Yet that perspective cannot fully define what it means to be a person since we are inevitably part of various social groups and institutions and cannot ignore the reality that much of our lives are peopled. What seems to happen is that, at moments, a more individual and separate sense of self emerges into our experiential foreground, while at others our individual self recedes into the background while a more interconnected sense of ourselves as a "person-in-relationship" emerges as primary. Barret-Lennard points to an emerging understanding that "Person-centered thought is transcending the philosophy of individualism in which it was rooted, while preserving its belief in the worth and dignity of each person" (Cooper et al., 2007, p. 135).

The view of persons as beings-in-relationship is especially relevant to how we understand our clients' problems. The most frequent reason clients seek psychotherapy is for problems in interpersonal relationships. These problems may take many forms, including depression, social anxiety, loneliness, paranoia, anger, extreme self-consciousness, conflicts with spouses or other people, and difficulties in acculturation, among others. Problems in relating to others, and especially the inability to form close and mutually supportive relationships, are common in our clients. Dean Ornish, author of *Love and Survival* (1997), has even dubbed loneliness, isolation, and depression as the "real epidemic in our culture," leading to a loss of "social structures that used to provide us with a sense of connection and community" (pp. 12–13).

Clearly, a large portion of the concerns clients bring to therapists are primarily interpersonal, and even problems that seem primarily intrapersonal (e.g., low self-esteem) often have interpersonal components.

Since problems in relating and lack of close and supportive relationships are at the core of many of our clients' problems, one could readily make the case that intimate relationships are good for one's sense of wellbeing and mental health. Ornish (1997) provides substantial evidence for the healing power of intimacy. One of the major conclusions of the research he reviewed was that anything that enhances one's sense of love, intimacy, connection, and community is good for our mental and physical health. Conversely, anything that promotes a sense of isolation often led to illness and suffering. Simple observation, experience, and common sense tell us that good relationships promote our sense of well-being, while poor relationships or a lack of relationships adversely affect our sense of well-being.

Given the interpersonal basis for our clients' sense of well-being or lack thereof, the quality of the therapist–client relationship becomes central to client adjustment and growth. Therefore, as Mearns and Cooper suggest, an optimal therapeutic relationship is one "in which dialogue and interaction take more center stage: one in which it is the *encounter* between the therapist and client, rather than the *provision* of a particular set of conditions *for* the client" (2005, p. 9). This approach enables the therapeutic relationship to serve as a "social learning lab" in which client and therapist collaborate as participants and observers who experiment with ways of engaging that enable the client to live more effectively in the moment and to take such experiences into other relationships.

DIALOGIC ASPECTS

All real living is meeting.

—Martin Buber (1958, p.11)

Increasingly, person-centered therapists such as Mearns and Cooper (2005) are incorporating into their work aspects of dialogical psychotherapy, defined by Buber scholar and psychotherapist Maurice Friedman as " a therapy that is centered on the meeting between the therapist and his or her client . . . as the central healing mode" (2002, p. 11). This "healing through meeting" is a two-person, bidirectional psychotherapy that emphasizes the authentic meeting or encounter between therapist and client. Consequently, self-actualization is viewed more as a byproduct of the quality of meeting between two persons rather than something one strives for by developing one's qualities or potentials. There is an intuitive wisdom to this notion as many persons, clients included, often attribute aspects of their growth to extraordinary experiences with a special person in their lives.

The healing through meeting of dialogic engagement means that the therapist's fundamental intent is to make meaningful and authentic contact with the client rather than trying to enable the client to be different or to achieve a specific outcome deemed desirable by the client or therapist. Instead, the client's spontaneous and authentic engagement with the therapist is supported, encouraged, and reciprocated. Such extraordinary meetings between therapist and client may take various forms and are often experienced as intense, novel, touching, intimate, loving, rich in personal learning, and unforgettable. For authentic meeting to have a therapeutic impact, the therapist needs to be fully *present* to and engaged with the client. As Yontef states: "A requirement of dialogic contact is the therapist's willingness to be 'genuine and unreserved' by honestly revealing anything that the therapist believes will enable the ongoing dialogue" (2007, p. 21).

Existential and gestalt therapists (e.g., Friedman, 1985; Yontef, 1993) identify inclusion as a critical component of dialogic encounter. Inclusion or "imagining the real" is an expanded empathic process during which the therapist imagines what the client is experiencing and grasps the client's unique being-in-the-world. Inclusion also represents the therapist's "bipolar experiencing of the other side of the relationship without leaving one's own ground" (Friedman, 1985, p. 199). In other words, the therapist remains a separate self and brings forth that self-existence and perspective in service of the client. Friedman contrasts inclusion with empathy, which "attempts to get over to the other while leaving oneself" (1985, p. 200). In inclusion, there is more mutuality in sharing than is usual in the classical person-centered style of empathic responding, which primarily limits itself to grasping and communicating the client's experiencing. Inclusion also

PERSON-CENTERED PSYCHOTHERAPIES

provides a means for a greater depth of relating and intimacy between client and therapist.

Therapist confirmation of the other is another powerful aspect of healing through meeting. It includes, but also goes beyond, acceptance by confirming clients as they are in the present as well as what they may become. For Jourard, "confirmation is an act of love through which one acknowledges the other as one who exists in his own peculiar form and has the right to do so" (Friedman, 1985, p.134). As Buber contends:

> Confirmation means . . . accepting the [other's] potentiality. . . .
> I not only accept the other as he is, but I confirm him, in myself and
> then in him, in relation to this potentiality that . . . can now be devel-
> oped. . . . "I accept you as you are" . . . does *not* mean "I don't want
> you to change," but . . . I discover in you just by my accepting love
> . . . what you are meant to become. (Friedman, 1985, pp. 135–136)

Thus, in dialogical encounter, the therapist first accepts clients as they are but also may confront and challenge them to become their potential. Friedman expanded on this notion when he said that the therapist "is not only concerned with the person [the client] is at that moment, but also with [the client] becoming what he or she is called to become":

> It is not that I judge you from above or that I moralize at you. Yet
> our relationship is a demand on you as on me. . . . The therapist
> may have to wrestle with the patient, for the patient and against
> the patient. He is not only concerned with the person he is at that
> moment, but also with his becoming what he or she is called to
> become. (1985, p. 137)

Another characteristic of dialogical engagement is a commitment to "the between," that which transpires between therapist and client. In this process, the therapist's perception is not privileged or considered objective or "truth" but is subject to change in the interaction. In other words, the therapist and client mutually influence each other, and both can be changed by the other. Thus, the therapist is willing to be vulnerable, accountable, and receptive to being affected by the client and does not hide behind a professional façade but instead meets "self to self." This does not negate the reality that the primary focus of the therapist is the client and the client's concerns or that each has different roles. While there are moments when both therapist and client benefit from the encounter, more often the commitment to the between primarily facilitates the process of the therapy.

One of the primary contributions of the dialogical approach is that it makes more room for therapists to bring relevant aspects of themselves to the client. The therapist also understands that each client has multiple selves that come forth at various moments, sometimes in discord with each other.

PLURALISTIC SELVES PERSPECTIVE

Rogers's conceptualization of the self or self-concept as a unitary phenomenon has been reexamined and refined by theorists. Some person-centered experts believe that a more accurate view is that individuals have multiple aspects of self that emerge in various moments and contexts. Cooper (2007) notes that these "multiple elements" may be variously conceived as "configurations of self," "modes of being," "inner persons," "subselves," "voices," or "parts" (p. 86). This altered view of the self has arisen as therapists noted that clients often refer to various parts of themselves.

Clients often articulate these various aspects of self or selves-in-conflict when they say such things as "part of me wants to be married while another part likes the freedom of being unattached." Sometimes clients speak of aspects of self that are related to specific roles (e.g., "I'm a good mother"). The regard clients hold for themselves may vary as different aspects of self emerge and become figural. For example, a client who has just expressed rage at his son feels ashamed, while that same client feels proud of a recent accomplishment as a scientist. The existence of multiple selves may be understood as a natural outcome of the complexity of human beings engaging in a vast variety of life experiences that produce physical, social, spiritual, cognitive, emotional, or psychological selves, among many other possibilities for being. From a narrative perspective stories are created, remembered, and told (and retold) that reflect specific qualities of self or ways of being. Each aspect of self may have varying experiences of the world. For example, a soldier whose religious values lead him to adopt a pro-life stance in terms of abortion may hold a view that it is fully justifiable to kill on the battlefield.

These various selves often communicate with each other in silent or overt self-dialogue. In simple terms, we often talk to ourselves as if we are relating to the different persons who exist within us. For example, a person who perceives himself to have acted immaturely may state, "When are you ever going to grow up?" One's diverse selves may exist in harmony or in conflict and may be isolated or integrated into a more cohesive sense of "I" or "me."

Stiles, a person-centered theorist, proposes an assimilation model in which people are construed "as composed of many pieces . . . [where] each piece consists of the traces of an experience or of a constellation of related experiences" (Watson et al., 2002, p. 406). Stiles refers to these experiences as voices and proposes that,

> The voice metaphor underlies our understanding that traces of experience—including problematic experiences—are active agents within people. That is, the voices can speak and act. . . . Theoretically, in successful therapy, a problematic, unwanted, outcast voice establishes contact with the dominant community of voices within a person, negotiates an understanding and is assimilated into the community. (Watson et al., 2002, p. 407)

These aspects of self, when problematic, are often polarized, antagonistic (e.g., "I hate this part of myself"), unaccepted (and unacceptable), and thus alienated from the lager sense of self. In order to more accurately grasp these various selves in the client, therapists need to shift their perspective from a unitary and executive self to one that recognizes the multiplicity of ways clients view and experience themselves at various moments. A challenge for clients and their therapists is to find ways to reconcile and integrate different aspects of the same person, especially when they are incongruent and in conflict with each other.

To summarize, there is no longer one form of person-centered therapy, although Rogers's "necessary and sufficient conditions" model is still the most widely known and accepted. Rogers himself recognized that there was no one way to practice person-centered therapy. He took the position that,

> The approach is paradoxical. It emphasizes shared values, yet encourages uniqueness. It is rooted in a profound regard for the wisdom and

constructive capacity inherent in the human organism—a regard that is shared by those who hold to this approach. At the same time, it encourages those who incorporate these values to develop their own special and unique ways of being, their own ways of implementing this shared philosophy. (1986, pp. 3–4)

Rogers expected person-centered therapy to continue to evolve and supported others in taking his ideas to the next levels. Developments in theory and corresponding advances in practice have been substantial in the last 25 years. Such progress is likely to continue as students of person-centered therapies continue to break new ground. This is as things should be in order for person-centered therapists of various persuasions to become increasingly more effective in assisting their clients.

In the next chapter, I will discuss how the theory of person-centered therapies might be put into practice and address the processes and mechanisms by which constructive change occurs.

4

The Therapy Process

In this chapter, I will begin with the paramount role of the therapist–client relationship, followed by the specific contributions of therapist and client, individually and collaboratively. Throughout the chapter I will attempt to articulate the various mechanisms of change that foster client growth.

ROLE OF THERAPIST–CLIENT RELATIONSHIP

One of the most fundamental premises of person-centered/humanistic psychotherapy is that an *optimal therapeutic relationship* is considered to be a primary source of constructive change in the client. A mutually engaged relationship between therapist and client often promotes growth in and of itself. When clients and therapists meet at relational depth, each often has an experience of how one can and might live with others. Through consistently good contact and extraordinary moments of encounter with their therapists, clients may experience themselves in ways that are rich, fresh, hopeful, and even transformative. Over time this quality of engagement with the therapist takes hold and is enacted in relationships with others. In addition to promoting constructive change in and of itself, the relationship provides an atmosphere conducive for intrapersonal and interpersonal learning.

In person-centered therapy, the core therapist qualities of empathy, unconditional positive regard, and congruence, enhanced by the therapist's presence, work synergistically and holistically to create a safe and supportive environment for learning and growth. Each therapist quality or condition augments the impact of the other. Before clients can feel accepted and valued, they must first perceive that their therapists "see" them clearly and have a sense of who they are, what it is like to be them and to live in their worlds. It is also essential that the client's sense of being accepted and prized be based in an experience that the therapist is congruent and trustworthy. Otherwise clients may feel that their therapist are simply "doing their job" by being accepting and trying to help them feel better or improve their self-esteem. These attitudes are enhanced to the degree that the therapist is fully present and immersed in the moment-to-moment unfolding of the client's world, and to the degree that the client is able to receive and absorb the therapist's regard. Person-centered therapists' optimism about their clients' resourcefulness and capacity to actualize their potential also creates a sense of hopefulness and encouragement that strengthens clients' beliefs that they can grow and effectively address their problems. The quality of the relationship is influenced as well by what the client brings to it since it is created and influenced by both therapist and client. Mutual affirmation between therapists and clients, in particular, creates a congenial and sup-portive atmosphere that enables clients to engage their courage to struggle with their issues.

As therapy proceeds, clients often internalize their therapists' attitudes of empathy, acceptance, and congruence. They learn to listen more sensitively to themselves and increase self-awareness and self-understanding. They gradually become less critical and more self-accepting as they incorporate their therapists' views of them. Clients learn to be more congruent as they see themselves more clearly and develop the courage to be known and to express thoughts and feelings they previously tended to withhold. Equally important, they become more empathic, accepting, and congruent in their relationships with others, thereby engaging others in more meaningful and satisfying ways.

Role of Therapist

When clients enter therapy, they often feel stuck in their lives and discouraged about their capacity to deal with others, themselves, or their problems. Feeling demoralized, they need a sense of hope and encouragement that their lives can be better. The person-centered therapist's natural optimism about clients' resourcefulness and capacity to change in a constructive manner often creates a glimmer of hope. As Rogers (1980) has stated, clients have within themselves resources for self-understanding and change. Therapists can activate these resources if they can provide a "definable climate of facilitative psychological attitudes" (p. 115). The "definable climate" includes the therapist's genuineness, transparency, or congruence; acceptance, nonjudgmental caring, prizing, affirmation, and unconditional positive regard; a genuine desire to understand the client's experience; and accurate empathic communication of that experience.

Other relational qualities and attitudes embraced by person-centered therapists include: a relationship characterized by trust, safety, and support; receptivity to experience; contact and engagement; immersion in the client's experience; a therapeutic alliance and authentic dialogue; and hopefulness regarding the client's capacity for constructive change. Other therapist attributes also contribute to the quality of the relationship. Qualities such as the therapist's encouragement, sense of humor, groundedness, tolerance for ambiguity, commitment to the client, respect, kindness, patience, courage, forthrightness, and integrity, among others, help create an optimal relationship. During the course of therapy, the sensitive therapist will bring forth any number of personal qualities and responses depending on what seems most relevant and therapeutic at a given time.

Person-centered therapists also serve, indirectly, as role models and "teachers" for their clients. Over time, clients observe their therapists' manner of engagement and living and begin to incorporate those qualities and behaviors into their own lives. In the next sections I will elaborate further the ways in which therapists have an impact on their clients.

Being Present

Person-centered therapists often refer to their therapeutic approach as a "way of being" with clients. An essential desire of the person-centered therapist is to *be present*, fully attentive to and immersed in the person of the client as well as the client's expressed concerns. By being present, the therapist completely brings the person he or she is to engage with the client. The therapist is receptive to whatever the client addresses and is responsive to the client's manner of communication, including verbal, nonverbal, affective, and body language. The therapist attends to and "takes in" the client's entire being and all modes of communication. Clients are usually quite aware of how present their therapists are with them, just as most of us are aware of how attentive and interested others are when we converse with them. Therapists, too, are aware of whether they are "going through the motions" of acting interested versus actually being invested in "being with" their clients. Therapist presence implies that the therapist is willing to be fully open to and affected by the client and willing to be actively responsive to the client. When therapists are fully present, clients often experience the impact of their therapists' being in a way that enhances their experience of their concerns and themselves. Presence underlies and enhances the impact of the therapist's manner of being and expression. It is often communicated nonverbally through body language (e.g., leaning forward, head nods), facial expression (e.g., quality of eye contact, concerned look), vocal tone (e.g., a tone that fits the client's emotional expression), and nonverbal communication (e.g., "m-hm m-hm").

Promoting Client Freedom

Another endeavor of the person-centered therapist is to support and encourage the client's freedom to choose what will be addressed, how it will be addressed, and what changes the client will decide to make. Thus, the person-centered therapist favors a nondirective style of engagement that encourages the client to decide what is important to talk about, believing the client knows best what "hurts" and what needs attention. At times, clients will request direction from the therapist in terms of what to talk about or what to do during the session or how to manage problematic aspects of their lives. While the person-centered therapist acknowledges the client's preference for such guidance, he or she will generally leave such decisions and responsibility with the client. Consequently, person-centered therapists tend to engage sparingly in making suggestions, giving advice, directing the content of the session, or otherwise attempting to influence the client's decisions. While the client is freed to engage in therapy in a manner that best suits him or her, the client is also faced with deciding what to share and how to manage his or her life, albeit it in a supportive relationship. Occasionally, clients have difficulty adjusting to the therapist's lack of directiveness, but most adjust and learn the value of self-reliance, making choices and being active participants in their therapy.

Being Accepting, Unconditional in Regard, and Affirming

Being accepted and valued for who one is is likely a universal need or desire. Maslow (1987) identified "love and belonging" as fundamental and basic needs that, if not met, lead to loneliness, alienation, ostracism, and a questioning of one's worth. People will go to great extremes to manage their public image in the hope of being perceived in a positive manner. For children, there are few experiences more damaging or painful than disapproval, rejection, or abuse by their parents. One of my clients, an African American male in his early 30s, disclosed how he never felt accepted by his mother, much less valued by her. He commented, "How am I supposed to feel good about myself when my own mother doesn't like me?" Long ago, Adler recognized how important it was for children (and adults) to have a sense of belonging and a place of value in their families and social groups. We are essentially social beings whose well-being depends largely on our feeling affiliated with, securely attached to, and loved by at least a few significant persons in our lives. A lack of, and need for, secure attachment is often evident in our clients.

The therapist's unconditional positive regard, acceptance, nonpossessive warmth, lack of judgment, and affirming attitudes and responses powerfully influence the client's view of self and sense of well-being. Mearns and Thorne (2007) state their belief that:

> The counselor who holds this attitude deeply values the humanity of her client and is not deflected in that valuing by any particular client behaviors. The attitude manifests itself in the counselor's consistent acceptance of and enduring warmth towards her client. (p. 95)

Lietaer offers a view of unconditionality as the therapist's "valuing the deepest core of the person, what she potentially is and can become" (p. 105). The person-centered therapist strives to maintain such sentiments regardless of how badly a client may behave toward others, something that may indeed prove challenging. As daunting as this may seem, especially when clients express negative feelings toward their therapists, most are able to hold their clients in regard by valuing the whole person, warts and all. Mearns and Thorne (2007) address this challenge for the therapist as follows:

> The client feels that the counselor values him consistently throughout their relationship, despite the fact that he may not value himself and even if the counselor does not approve of all the client's behavior. It is possible to accept the client as a person of worth while still not liking some of the things he does. (p. 96)

To achieve such deep and pervasive acceptance, therapists themselves need to experience positive self-regard despite their own imperfections. By doing so, the therapist understands at a personal level that all persons are worthy *and flawed* and deserving of acceptance.

Occasionally therapists, especially those in the early stages of development, simply dislike or disapprove of clients for any number of reasons. Clients who mistreat others (e.g., physically abusive parents or spouses) may be particularly challenging for the neophyte therapist to accept. Similarly, many clients engage in a variety of behaviors that alienate others, the therapist included. In such cases, therapists' nonacceptance may be tempered by their understanding that their clients' negative behaviors usually have a constructive intent if viewed from the client's perspective. For example, a parent who harshly disciplines a child by yelling at or hitting the child may have the constructive intent of helping the child "learn important life lessons." When the therapist grasps the parent's intent, he or she is often able to feel more tolerant. When therapists find themselves disliking particular clients, it may help to recall that what they dislike represents a part but not nearly all that the client is. It may also help therapists to remind themselves that their dislike is *theirs* and may reflect their own biases or issues. Most everyone has redeeming qualities, and the empathic therapist is likely to locate and embrace such qualities if he or she remains receptive to all aspects of the client. It also helps to embrace the view that all persons, no matter how badly they have behaved, are redeemable. One of the reasons Dickens' *A Christmas Carol* is so compelling is that it conveys the message that we all have the potential to redeem ourselves at any point in our lives, no matter what we may have done.

Therapists' positive regard for their clients has a number of constructive effects on the therapeutic relationship and client growth. Clients usually come to therapy when they are distressed, "stuck" and discouraged that what they're doing isn't working. One thing most all clients hope for is someone with whom they feel comfortable, someone they like and feel accepts them as they are. Because so many clients come to therapy with low self-esteem, self-doubt, shame, and insecurity, their therapists' genuine acceptance provides safety and comfort that enables them to open up and disclose problematic and unattractive aspects of themselves. Therapists' acceptance reduces threat, defensiveness, and clients' inclination to be self-protective, which, in turn, enables clients to be more open to all of their experiences and be more involved in therapy. As clients realize that they are seen for whom they are *and* valued, they may revise the views they have of themselves in more positive directions and become more self-accepting. Previously introjected conditions of worth from significant others (e.g., "I am acceptable if . . .") are counteracted and reduced as clients experience and absorb the therapist's regard for them, as well as the regard from others that was previously dismissed because it was felt to be undeserved. Similarly, clients become less susceptible to the harsh internal judgment of their personal "critic." Gradually, the locus of evaluation shifts from others to self and from critical self to more tolerant self. Consequently, clients may feel less compelled to act in a certain manner to be acceptable to others (and the critic) and gradually learn to make self-statements along the line of "I am OK the way I am, including my limitations and flaws." Further, clients often learn to value their own way of being in the world, even if it is not acceptable to their significant others. In other words, their locus of evaluation shifts from an external to an internal one as clients gain courage to be who they are and accept the consequences. As Rogers has noted, "It takes courage to live" and be true to oneself. Increased self-acceptance seems to beget increased tolerance and acceptance of others, which often results in more congenial and intimate relationships. When clients feel more positively about themselves, they seem to approach life with greater equanimity and tolerate life's challenges and disappointments more effectively.

While the nonjudgmental empathy of the person-centered therapist tends to communicate acceptance indirectly, therapist affirmation is a more active and overtly positive form of validating and valuing the client. Therapist acceptance, regard, and affirmation are sentiments that often need to be expressed tangibly to the client to have optimal therapeutic effect. Such expression may take many forms such as smiling, warm vocal tone, consistent eye contact, shared laughter, celebrating the client's triumphs, looking pleased to see the client, self-disclosure about something the therapist values in the client (e.g., "you are a loving mother") among many others. In his well-known session with Gloria (Rogers, Perls, & Ellis, 1965), Rogers spontaneously commented, "You look to be a pretty nice daughter," a comment that obviously touched her. In a recent session with a client, I commented, "You're a person I'd like to have for a brother, a friend, or a son." The client indicated that he greatly appreciated this affirmation, especially because he felt I knew him well. It is important that affirmations are made congruently and without manipulative intent, lest they be experienced as superficial attempts to "make the client feel better." As clients become aware that their therapists value their strengths and personal qualities, they are able, to varying degrees, to view themselves in a more accurate and positive light. As clients feel better about themselves, they often gain confidence to try out new behaviors.

Finally, I think the issue of touching as a form of supportive contact with clients deserves clarification. Touching is a natural part of engaging with and expressing support and affection for another person. Such touching has a place in therapy as long as it is clearly nonsexual and nonexploitative in intent. Shaking a client's hand, touching a client on the shoulder, an encouraging pat on the back or arm, or hugging one's client on occasion are all appropriate means of expressing one's caring and support for the client. Therapists must, of course, be clear about their motives for touching their clients and only touch clients when their intent is benign, natural, and clearly of therapeutic intent. In addition, clients must be receptive to being touched. Conversely, if the therapist has misgivings about touching the client, he or she should probably refrain from doing so. The bottom line is that therapeutic touch must be a genuine expression of caring and support and be experienced as such by the client.

Clients themselves often initiate touch with their therapists. They may wish to shake hands at the beginning or end of their sessions or sometimes touch their therapists during the session. For example, I have had clients touch my arm or knee in a friendly manner as we talked. Some clients seek hugs from their therapists, most often after difficult sessions. The vast majority of clients touch their therapists in a natural and innocent manner. If therapists understand touch as a natural way of expressing appreciation, support, or appropriate affection between therapists and clients, then it will almost inevitably have a constructive impact.

Being Authentic, Genuine, Transparent

Being genuine or congruent means that the therapist is what he or she seems to be. What the therapist experiences internally is matched by his or her words, behavior, feelings, and manner of expression. Therapist genuineness lends credibility to everything the therapist does. Congruent therapists are more likely to be perceived as trustworthy and honest and as persons of integrity. When the therapist is transparent, or willing to be known, and without deception of any kind or intent to act like someone he or she is not, the client is likely to feel trusting. Conversely, incongruence on the part of the therapist may cause the client to be cautious or guarded. Congruent therapists do not play the role of therapist or hide behind it but are naturally themselves in relationship to their clients. In simple terms the person-centered therapist eschews any form of deception, phoniness, or manipulative behavior no matter how benign in intent. They have little or no need to hold back anything that is relevant to their clients. At times, the person-centered therapist may invite the client to inquire about the therapist's comments, behavior, or his or her thoughts or feelings about the client. Such openness is often vital to clients who tend not to trust others or misread others' intentions. Recently, one of my clients expressed her deep distrust of most people, fearing that they would attempt to take advantage of her. She seemed hypersensitive to some of my physical gestures (e.g., rubbing my brow) and expressed her concern that I may be withholding something from her. I encouraged her to check with me about anything I said or did and assured her that I would let her know my thoughts and reactions to her. She greatly appreciated this opportunity and did inquire a few times about some nonverbal behavior that she feared signaled a lack of interest in her. My willingness to be open with her enabled her to be more trusting of me.

Rogers came to believe that therapist congruence was the most important element in therapy:

> It is when the therapist is natural and spontaneous that he seems to be most effective. . . . Our experience has deeply reinforced and extended my view that the person who is able *openly* to be himself in that moment, as he is at the deepest levels he is able to be, is the effective therapist. Perhaps nothing else is of any importance. (Rogers & Stevens, 1967, pp. 188–189)

Clearly, this was a radical position that challenged the prevailing views of how therapists comport themselves with their clients. Far from the position of classical psychoanalysis where therapists were to remain neutral and unknown so their clients could project interpersonal conflicts onto their therapists via transference reactions, Rogers's view was that authentic encounter with the client was itself therapeutic.

There are numerous ways the therapist's congruence contributes to the change process. As mentioned earlier, having a meaningful encounter with a congruent and present therapist often has a therapeutic impact on the client. Clients sometimes learn to be more congruent through authentic engagement with the therapist since realness on the part of the therapist often begets realness in the client. When there is a genuine meeting between therapist and client, both are enriched by the quality of contact. Clients then have the experience that they can engage meaningfully with the therapist and, by extension, other persons. Therapist self-disclosure that is relevant to a client's experience (e.g., the pain of losing a pet) often helps the client feel understood and less alone in his or her troubling feelings. When therapists are transparently real, clients see that they are persons just like others instead of omnipotent or omniscient beings. This often provides perspective for clients and enables them to become more self-accepting.

Although it may not be therapists' intent, they often serve as models of an authentic manner of being for the client. Through vicarious learning, clients see and experience what it means to be authentic and try out for themselves more transparent ways of engaging with others. Consequently, the quality of their primary and everyday relationships is often enriched. They learn that it can be gratifying to be open with others who, in turn, are more likely to be open with them. Communication is generally enhanced because it is more direct and honest and, therefore, less subject to image management, political correctness, deception, qualification, caution, and the myriad ways that communication can be compromised.

Congruent therapists may use themselves in a variety of ways on behalf of their clients. Although person-centered therapists tend to focus primarily on their clients' lived experience, there are times when they respond spontaneously as the person they are. By doing so, they often bring forth aspects of themselves that are intended to serve their clients. Clearly, various qualities of the therapist other than empathy and unconditional regard are often therapeutic. In any given course of therapy, the particular relational qualities that may be growth enhancing will inevitably vary. Just as the client can be understood in terms of a variety of selves that may emerge at different moments in varying contexts, so can the therapist. For example, the therapist may engage his or her sense of humor with the client, make affirmative comments, or even challenge the client as long as such behaviors are intended to foster the therapeutic relationship, process, or the client's goals and well-being.

Being congruent doesn't mean that person-centered therapists have license to say or do whatever they feel, simply because it is an honest response. It is essential that the therapist's genuineness be relevant to the client and the current therapeutic situation and be of constructive intent. Congruent expressions of the therapist can be a problematic, and sometimes risky, endeavor. Expressions of congruence may be harmful and damaging to the therapeutic relationship. For example, expressing anger at a client for lack of effort during or between sessions may be authentic but runs a high risk of being harmful and should generally be avoided. In the Gloria series of sessions, Perls was rated high on authenticity but was experienced by Gloria as alienating (Rogers et al., 1965).

Congruent expression of the self of the therapist means that the therapist's words, actions, feelings, thoughts, and intents are an integrated whole. Since congruent expressions of the self may be for better or worse, such expressions need to be made judiciously. Keep in mind that research indicates that therapist congruent expressions are sometimes negatively related to client outcome. Discriminating expression of self is certainly called for in the therapeutic endeavor. Therefore I offer some guidelines for the congruent expression or use of self in the form of questions therapists might ask themselves.

Guideline 1: *Is my authentic expression intended to be in the best interest of my client?* An affirmative answer to this question usually indicates that the therapist is of good will and intention. It also suggests that the response is believed to have therapeutic value.

Guideline 2: *Is my congruent expression relevant to the immediate therapeutic situation?* Therapists sometimes succumb to the impulse to share aspects of their lives, feelings, or thoughts that are not relevant to the immediate therapeutic situation. Thus, therapists should ask themselves, "Does this fit?" or "Is this relevant to the client's concerns?"

Guideline 3: *Is my expression natural, spontaneous, authentic, and without any hidden or manipulative intent?* If the therapist feels awkward, hesitant, uncertain, uncomfortable, or in any way incongruent, then he or she would probably be wise to refrain from personal expression. Further, if the therapist has the sense that he or she may be "up to something" that is not clear or is uncertain whether his or her motives may be deceptive, compromised, or possibly manipulative, then the therapist would do well to contain such responses.

Guideline 4: *When strains or problems in the therapeutic relationship arise and persist, is my response intended to understand, constructively address, and repair such problems?* Strains in the therapeutic relationship are not uncommon and often derail the therapy. Unfortunately, clients often do not share their problematic reactions to the therapist or therapeutic process. Therefore, the burden of addressing such strains or rifts falls to the therapist. At times, when the therapist is having difficulty with a client, he or she may disclose his or her feelings or concerns in an attempt to resolve any problems that may exist in the relationship. Rogers used as a marker any *persistent* problematic reaction or feeling elicited by the client as an impetus to share his own feelings or perceptions with his client. Therapists need to be aware of their possible contributions to the strains and nondefensive in acknowledging their part in them. When therapists are the main source of the strain, it is appropriate for the therapist to acknowledge this and apologize to the client.

Guideline 5: *When I have negative reactions toward my client, do I first consider that such responses may reflect problematic issues of my own?* When therapists react negatively to clients, I believe it is valuable to remember that not all therapists or others familiar with the client would have an adverse reaction. Thus, therapists should first look at themselves and consider that their own biases, blind spots, or problems may be at play.

Guideline 6: *Would the client be better served by my withholding some of my feelings and reactions, especially if such expressions have the potential to be hurtful to or burden the client or damage our relationship?* The psychotherapist's commitment should be to "first do no harm." When therapists have moderate to strong doubts about the effects of their disclosure, it is often wise to refrain from or postpone sharing their reactions. If the therapist's response is likely to elicit defensiveness, hurt the client's feelings, or damage the relationship, then the therapist should probably refrain from such expression.

Guideline 7: *When I decide to share negative or problematic reactions to my client, is my intent clearly to be of therapeutic benefit?* There are times when therapists' reactions to clients are "diagnostic" in the sense that they likely represent responses that would be common to other therapists and other persons who know the client. For example, a client who complains of a lack of intimate relations may disclose relatively little of a personal nature and tend to focus on superficial aspects of her life. The therapist might notice his or her reaction to such a client and share that he or she feels disconnected from the client. In doing so, the therapist's intent would be to use the immediate situation to explore with the client how his or her manner of relating seems to interfere with the development of closeness. When therapists make such observations and decide to share them, it is essential that the therapist feels benign and constructive in his or her intent.

In sum, each therapist needs to be attuned to the personal characteristics and emerging needs of the client and bring forth aspects of the self that foster relational engagement, deal with conflicts, and address relational strains or ruptures. If therapists consistently ask themselves, "Is my response intended to be in the bests interests of my client?" they will likely make sound decisions most of the time.

Being Empathic

The simple act of our listening communicates caring and interest. Conversely, having the experience of not being heard or, worse, being ignored or misunderstood is often frustrating and alienating. When clients talk about therapy, they often speak about how important it is to "have someone to talk to," "get it out," "get it off my chest," or "have a neutral person to discuss things with." In fact, clients identify being understood as one of the most helpful aspects of their therapists and express deep appreciation for being listened to so carefully.

A defining endeavor of person-centered therapists is to attend to the client with all of their senses and to seek to understand the client's world, especially what it is like to be the client. This is active and involved listening in which the therapist attempts to communicate as clearly and precisely as possible the client's reality, including its nuances and that which is implicit. In this endeavor, the therapist is a learner who sets aside any possible biases, assumptions, or preconceptions and listens with fresh ears and sees with fresh eyes to take in the client as he or she is. In a sense, through empathic attunement the therapist meditates on the person of the client and his or her experience. This enables clients to meditate on themselves. The therapist communicates as clearly as possible his or her understanding of the client's thoughts and experiences for the client to reflect upon and process further. In a sense the therapist attempts to paint a vivid, living, multicolored portrait of the client's immediate experience. Doing so enables clients to listen to and see themselves more clearly and make better sense of their experiences and themselves.

Sometimes person-centered therapy is misunderstood or caricatured as the therapist simply saying back or restating what the client has just said. This was never Rogers's intent nor was it reflected in his behavior. Instead, the person-centered therapist seeks to understand both the stated and intended message of the client, including the tacit meanings that may only be hinted at or on the edge of awareness. In a sense, person-centered therapists hold up a "magical mirror" for their clients that enables them to experience themselves and their perceptions, feelings, and beliefs more freshly and with greater clarity than was previously possible. Although there are inevitably times when therapists do not understand their clients or understand them incompletely, they remain steadfast in striving to grasp the client's world more accurately. Early on in my career I worked with an adolescent who was struggling with the realization that he was gay. I did my best to understand his struggles and to lend my support. After one session he said to me in an appreciative manner, "You are the only person who understands me, or at least tries to." I have long held on to this learning that our clients appreciate our imperfect efforts to understand them. Therapists, even experienced ones, often underestimate the importance of just listening to and receiving their clients. Sometimes beginning therapists get caught up in feeling they must "do something" and initiate premature attempts at problem solving because they fail to understand that their caring presence and empathic responsiveness are therapeutic in and of themselves for most clients.

In whimsical moments, I have imagined that the Psychotherapy Police, in their frustration with the overproliferation of untested and questionable therapy methods, insist that each therapist choose and stick with one primary therapeutic response that is supported by clinical evidence and research. If limited by such an injunction, my one therapeutic endeavor would be to listen and share that understanding. "First seek to understand" would be a worthy mantra for therapists of any persuasion. Psychotherapy research studies (e.g., Watson et al., 2002) indicate that therapist empathy usually shows a positive relationship to client outcome while no studies of therapist empathy show a negative relationship, suggesting that empathy is never harmful. In 30 years of experience, I have never had a client complain about being understood.

Defining Empathy. Webster's dictionary defines empathy as "the act of understanding, being aware of, being sensitive to, and vicariously experiencing the feelings, thoughts and experience of another and communicating them to another." As defined by Rogers, being empathic is to "perceive the internal frame of reference of another with accuracy, and with the emotional components and meanings which pertain thereto, as if one were the other person, but without ever losing the 'as if' condition" (1959, p. 210). It implies entering another's world so completely as to have a sense of what it is like to be the other—how the other feels, thinks, and moves through life.

Empathy is a complex phenomenon composed of attitudes, values, skills, and behaviors. It is an *attitude* or readiness to respond in which the therapist has a desire to hear and understand the client. It is a *value* or ideal in the sense that it views others as worth knowing and deserving to be heard without bias or prejudgment. Empathy is a *complex skill* that requires focused attention and concentration, the ability to decode another's experience and encode that experience into clear and precise language. It is a *relational skill* that entails the capacity to be with, sensitively hear, and engage nonjudgmentally with the client. To a large degree, empathy is the effective use of one's imagination in that one bridges to the other by imagining the other's lived experience well enough to grasp and articulate it. It is sometimes a skill that draws on one's intuition to get a "feel for" or a "sense of" the other. Empathy requires discipline in focus and in resisting other less productive ways of responding to one's client. Empathy is a *behavior* in the sense that it is an active response that communicates one's understanding of another. Research (Watson, 2002) has identified a number of behavioral correlates of therapist empathy. They include: (a) direct eye contact and a concerned expression; (b) acknowledging head nods, leaning forward, and "uhm hms"; (c) an emotionally involved vocal tone that communicates interest and a level of emotional involvement and intensity that matches what the client is feeling; and (d) clear and precise language and use of emotional words. Interestingly, what clients experience as empathic is strongly affected by the therapist's body language, especially aspects that communicate presence, focus, and intense interest. Clearly, the expression of empathy is holistic in that it includes, but goes beyond, verbal expression of understanding. Negative correlates of empathy include: (a) a bored or detached vocal tone or one that has a sing-song quality, (b) interruptions, and (c) advice and reassurance (Watson et al., 2002). One might note that clients perceive as nonempathic well-intended behaviors of therapists such as advising and reassuring.

Relational Benefits of Empathy. Therapists should have sound reasons for whatever they do. Therefore, I will address the fundamental questions: "Why be empathic?" and "What is the therapeutic value of this way of being?" Both experience and research suggest that there are multiple constructive therapeutic effects for our clients. I will begin with the effects of empathy on the quality of the therapeutic relationship. First and primary, empathy creates a sanctuary that provides safety for clients to be themselves. Empathy is inherently nonjudgmental as it addresses what is, not what should be. When heard without evaluation, clients feel safe to disclose difficult aspects of themselves openly and nondefensively. As clients feel seen, respected, and valued, a feeling of closeness and a bond begins to develop between therapist and client. This bond helps create a sense of "weness" and mutuality, a feeling that "we're in this together," which in turn enhances cooperativeness and collaboration. Mutual liking often occurs as therapist and client come to know each other. Clients frequently feel hopeful and optimistic because someone else understands them, thereby removing a sense of alienation or isolation that comes from feeling different, strange, or hopelessly impaired or damaged.

Empathy, the Self and the Process of Change. Therapist empathy has numerous and far-reaching effects on intrapersonal learning. As clients are accurately heard by their therapists, they learn to reflect on their experience and engage in self-exploration that often leads to self-discovery, self-understanding, and altered views of the self. Michael Mahoney, author of *Human Changes Processes* (1991), astutely notes that "all psychotherapies are psychotherapies of the self" (p. 235). The self is central to how things are perceived as experiences are perceived primarily in relation to one's personal existence. A major benefit of person-centered therapy is that it facilitates self-definition by enabling clients to achieve greater clarity about who they are as opposed to who they thought they were. As clients come to see themselves in new ways, they are more likely to act in a manner consistent with the revised ways they see themselves.

During the course of therapy, clients become increasingly aware of experiences and behavior that they have kept from awareness or distorted by various defensive strategies designed to protect the self from being threatened or changed too rapidly. Being heard nonjudgmentally fosters clients' receptivity while reducing defensiveness, thereby enabling clients to muster their courage to "take a fearless inventory" and look at unpleasant and unacceptable aspects of themselves. As those aspects are accepted, they can be integrated into the current structure of the self. Paradoxically, as clients accept and integrate negative views of themselves, they seem to diminish in their impact because they no longer deny or defend undesirable qualities or behaviors, nor do they criticize or feel ashamed of themselves.

Most clients have a gap between the person they imagine themselves to be and the person they'd like to become. As clients experience an affirming and understanding relationship with their therapist, they often begin to see themselves through the therapist's eyes. The gap begins to close as the revised view of self comes closer to the ideal self. As clients develop their potential, they become more confident in the current view of self and learn to appreciate more aspects of themselves. They become their own locus of evaluation and are less dependent on others to affirm their worth. In other words, they learn to generate positive self-regard from within.

Empathy promotes reflection in all areas of clients' lives. As clients become more mindful, they come to trust increasingly their perceptions and judgment. They learn to see old things in new ways and increase their perceptual range and complexity as narrow views are expanded and differentiated. Consequently, they learn to deconstruct ingrained worldviews and create newer and more functional ones. This often leads to a sense of hope and optimism as clients realize that they need not remain stuck in old beliefs and behaviors. Clients become more adept at making sense of their experiences and achieving clarity about the implications of their intrapersonal and interpersonal learning and to become more effective decision makers and problem solvers. They learn to become their own therapists.

The Varieties of Empathy

In this section I will identify some of the various forms empathy might take. *Silent listening* often has a comforting effect on clients, allowing them to say what's on their mind in their own pace and manner. Cindy was a client who wanted me to listen without responding while she told me the entire story of her marriage and divorce. And so I did, for several weeks, carefully recording everything she said. Later, we returned to her story and processed the experience in detail. In an evaluation of my therapy with her, she described me as a "fantastic listener." Intent and patient listening is a form of attending to or ministering to another. This is an involved form of listening, not a passive one, that is often therapeutic in and of itself. The primary limitations of silent empathy are that therapists do not give their clients a response to interact with, nor do clients know if they have truly been understood.

Empathic understanding responses are the staple of the person-centered therapist in that they attempt to grasp and accurately communicate the client's basic message. This is the fundamental or basic form of empathy upon which more complex forms of empathy are built. These deceptively simple responses often lead clients to explore further what is currently present for them. They help set in motion and sustain clients' attention to relevant aspects of their experience.

C: I am just dragging today.

T: Just no energy for anything.

C: No, I just feel like staying home and avoiding everything I have to do.

Clarification is a form of empathy in which the therapist articulates clearly what the client is attempting to say, struggling to find words for, or expresses in a vague way. It brings into focus what the client means. Using a musical metaphor, it is as if the client hits a note off key and the therapist hits the right note. The client experiences a "ring of truth" and clarity.

C: I'm really out of sorts.

T: You seem angry.

C: I guess I am. Nothing is going right today!

Affective empathy focuses on the client's emotion or bodily felt sense of a problem. It goes beyond the content of the client's messages and articulates the feeling that is expressed or implied.

C: I just can't believe my mother is dead.

T: You're feeling sad and lost that she's no longer with you.

C: Terribly.

Explorative empathy uses a probing and tentative style as the therapist attempts to assist the client to locate, explore, unfold, examine, and reflect on unclear or hidden aspects of experience. The exploration might take the form or broadening or deepening the clients' understandings of their realities.

C: I can't quite put my finger on it, but I feel anxious about my upcoming wedding to Jim.

T: So there's some vague sense of doubt or fear about marrying Jim?

C: Yes. Like I'm not sure that he and I have the same hopes for our life together.

Evocative empathic responses are designed to heighten, make more vivid, amplify, and bring to life clients' experiences. The therapist uses rich, penetrating, connotative language, feeling words and imagery, and a dramatic expressive manner that heightens the client's experience. Accurately capturing the full feeling tone is especially important as the therapist strives to grasp the full impact of the client's experience.

C: (recalling being mugged)

T: You were scared to death he was going to shoot you. The hairs on your neck stood up as you felt the cold gun barrel on your neck and heard a threatening voice saying "Give me your wallet or you will never see another day."

C: That still sends shivers down my spine.

Inferential empathy endeavors to infer the meaning of something the client has hinted at or has stated at a more superficial level; it articulates the tacit or implicit in what is said. In this form of empathy, the therapist often articulates what is unspoken but at the edge of awareness, relying on his or her intuition and therapeutic judgment to do so. The veracity of the understanding is confirmed by the client's sense of its rightness.

C: (a professional tennis player) I played the worst game of my life in the final of my last tournament.

T: I know that leaves you profoundly disappointed in yourself, and I sense that you have tapped into your worst fears that you cannot perform under pressure.

C: Ugh. That's it! I just couldn't overcome my fear that I was going to screw up. Then I tightened up and lost all confidence. And *did* play poorly.

Affirmative empathic responses validate the client's experience or sense of self, whether positive or negative. To be optimally effective, such responses require credible evidence from the therapist's and client's knowledge of the client.

C: I am so proud of how my children are doing. I think I'm a good mother.

T: You are a good mother.

C: I think I've been neglectful of my husband.

T: From what you've said, I can see that you have been neglectful lately.

Empathic challenges are responses by therapists that address clients' perceptions and assumptions. While still acknowledging and remaining within the client's frame of reference, empathic challenges gently offer an alternative understanding or perspective—a different way of viewing the client's world, offering an opportunity for the client and therapist to work toward the best understanding possible.

C: I don't want to go to work today.

T: I think you *do* want to go to work but just not have to deal with your boss.

C: I guess that's true. I do like my work, just not working for my boss.

Conjectural or hypothetic empathy expresses the therapist's attempt to get at that which is out of or at the fuzzy edge of the client's awareness. The therapist provides an interpretation of the client's reality but does not attempt to provide new information. The therapist's response is grounded in the client's disclosures even though the information may not be in the foreground of the client's consciousness. Such responses often reflect something the therapist grasps that has not yet been articulated by the client but which is easily recognizable if accurate. Adlerian therapists have identified a mechanism called the *recognition reflex* that suggests that people naturally recognize a personal truth when it is clearly presented. The therapist might offer a hypothesis by saying something like "I have an idea of what might be going on. Would you like to hear my understanding?" The client almost inevitably is curious to hear what the therapist sees and readily accepts the invitation. The therapist then frames the response in a tentative manner by saying "Could it be that . . . ?" or "Is it possible that . . . ?" and then offers his or her understanding. By framing the conjecture or hypothesis in this manner, it is easily rejected if inaccurate. When it is accurate, the client resonates with it and confirms it.

C: I just don't know what to make of Kate's irritability toward me lately.

T: I have a thought about what may be going on. Would you like to hear my conjecture?

C: Yes.

T: Could it be that you have some fears that she doesn't accept you as you are?

C: Yes. That's it. I guess I didn't want to admit that.

Observational empathy is a response to nonverbal modes of communication such as facial expression, vocal tone, and body language. Observational empathy often takes the form of process observations regarding the client's manner of expression. Such responses often heighten clients' self-awareness and help them recognize that what they experience and communicate often goes beyond their words.

C: I can't believe how mean my mother can be.

T: I notice that your hand is all balled up in a fist as you talk about your mother.

C: I guess I am very angry at her.

Self-disclosure may serve to show that therapists grasp their clients' realities by sharing their own experiences. Such responses are often desirable when clients experience something that they doubt anyone else can possibly understand and often concern something powerful, like the feeling of the loss of a cherished pet.

C: When my dog died, I felt like a large piece of me died with him.

T: I think I do have some sense of how devastating that still is for you. When my dog died, I felt a terrible sense of sadness and loss. Like one of my best friends was gone.

C: Exactly.

First person empathy is a style in which the therapist speaks in the first person *as if* he or she were the client. Such responses have the effect of being more personal and impactful since clients hear their own voices spoken.

C: I am so depressed I can barely get out of bed.

T: I feel almost completely immobilized.

C: I just have no energy or desire to do anything.

A variation of first-person empathy is similar to the psychodrama method of "doubling" in which the therapist tries to inhabit the person of the client. It has its roots in an acting approach in which the actor seemingly *becomes* the person he or she is playing. In this approach to empathy, the therapist sits next to the client, with minimal eye contact in order to focus completely on the immediate, lived experiences of the client. In such moments, the therapist essentially is the client and speaks the client's voice. The therapist also allows himself or herself some "creative license" to express something outside of or on the edge of the client's awareness or to express something in a more dramatic way that the client has understated. Clients often report the powerful impact of hearing themselves speak; they say they get a more poignant sense of themselves. One of my clients expressed her appreciation for having the opportunity to have a "clone" of herself. She felt her true self was brought to life, and this enabled her to see and hear herself in a fresh way. In this style the therapist continuously checks with the client to verify the accuracy of his or her articulated understanding of the client.

C: I can't believe my husband cheated on me.

T: I feel crushed and betrayed.

C: That bastard! How could he do that?

T: I hate him for violating my trust.

C: I guess I do. I'm furious.

There are many other ways to communicate understanding to our clients, limited only by the therapist's imagination, creativity, and use of self. Sometimes empathy emerges from the therapist's intuitive sense of how to respond and takes unusual forms. For example, a therapist hears a client's feeling of being overwhelmed and comments, "Stop the world. I want to get off." Improvisational forms of empathy are often spontaneous and novel expressions of understanding. On many occasions I have sung a verse from a song to a client that captures the essence of the experience. A client of mine was talking about the difficulty of living with her boyfriend and I sang, "I don't know how to love him." Empathy might take simple forms such as offering a client a cup of tea when the therapist notices how stressed the client feels. Sometimes the form of empathy might be surprising and penetrating. For example, respected client-centered therapist John Shlien told of a client who was struggling with painful issues regarding his mother, to which Shlien responded, "Mama! Mama!" The client resonated strongly to Shlien's response. In sum, therapists and clients may find a wide variety of empathic responses to be effective.

Empathy and Emotion. Working empathically with clients' emotions is at the heart of effective therapy. Most of the problems clients experience are emotional in nature (e.g., depression, anxiety) or have a strong emotional component (e.g., conflicted relationships, low self-esteem). The "body knows" more than can be articulated, and finding the potential wisdom contained in clients' feelings often leads them forward. Our emotions have a number of important functions. They (a) reflect the body's interpretation of a situation or experience; (b) alert us to what's wrong or right, good or bad for us and orient us toward what's needed for our well-being; (c) represent impulses to act and serve to energize and prioritize action; (d) contain personal wisdom essential to effective functioning and growth; (e) reveal a meaning system that informs us of the importance of events in our lives; (f) often serve as precognitive means of adaptation enabling us to respond quickly to events; (g) help identify core beliefs or schemas; (h) help us clarify our motivation; (i) often serve as "wake-up calls" to attend to how one's life is not working; and (j) are critical to sound decision making.

Rather than view emotion primarily as something that interferes with functioning, person-centered/humanistic therapists have embraced the importance of understanding the adaptive nature of emotion in effective decision making and functioning. Neuroscientist Antonio Damasio, author of *Descartes' Error,* provides evidence that "certain aspects of the process of emotion and feeling are indispensable for rationality [and] . . . take us to the appropriate place in a decision-making space, where we may put the instruments of logic to good use" (1994, p. xiii). One cannot know oneself or function well in the world without paying attention to one's feelings. Conversely, an impairment in persons' ability to access emotional information disconnects them from one of their most adaptive meaning production systems and impairs their ability to make sense of the world.

A sizable and growing body of research shows that working with client emotion, and that depth of experiencing in particular, is consistently related to good client outcome (e.g., Greenberg, Korman, & Pavio, 2002). However, most clients do not tend to process their feelings uninvited, while some prefer to avoid them. Since clients often express emotions without attending to them, it is especially important for the therapist to point to what is felt, or on the edge of awareness, and invite the client to attend to it with curiosity and discover its personal meaning and implications. Further, as Sachse and Elliott (2002) have reported, the quality of the therapist's empathic response to the client may deepen, maintain, or diminish client's experiential processing and self-exploration. In short, when therapists deepen their responses, clients deepen theirs, but when therapists flatten their responses to emotion, so do clients. Finally, it is important to underscore that both *emotional expression and reflection* on the experienced emotion are critical for client change. The mere expression of emotion, while possibly cathartic, typically does not lead to functional learning unless the client cognitively processes the implied meaning of the emotion and its implications for more effective living.

Role of the Client

When Rogers articulated his "necessary and sufficient conditions" hypothesis, he specified only two conditions for the client: that the client and therapist are in psychological contact and that the client be "in a state of incongruence, being vulnerable or anxious" (1957, p. 96). Rogers believed that if clients experienced anxiety, or incongruence between their experiences and self-concepts, they would be sufficiently motivated to alleviate distress. This belief is also grounded in Rogers's assumption of an inherent master motivation, the actualizing tendency, which serves to maintain and enhance the organism. Rogers's concept of an organismic valuing process, a trustworthy evaluative mechanism that enables persons to experience satisfaction in behaviors that serve the person's growth, was seen as a source of wisdom in the client. The concept of "psychological contact" meant to Rogers that at least a minimal relationship between therapist and client existed, one in which therapist and client make a perceived difference in the field of the other. He stated his belief that "significant personality change does not occur except in a relationship" (1957, p. 96). Rogers's faith was that *if* certain specifiable therapist qualities were experienced by the client, *then* the actualizing tendency would propel the client toward growth and psychological health.

As in any therapy, the client's responsibility is to identify and discuss meaningful concerns and problems. As clients do so and experience their therapists' nonjudgmental empathy, they tend to elucidate their issues further, explore and reflect on them, and assess how new learnings and insights might be applied to their daily lives. Since person-centered therapy is fundamentally nondirective, it is the client's responsibility to determine the direction of therapy and how to participate. Since person-centered therapy is basically a relational therapy, clients are likely to benefit to the degree that they engage effectively with their therapists. Clients' willingness to express their feelings and process them is also a critical client task. In addition, it is the client's responsibility to make the choice to change and the effort to incorporate change in their daily lives.

Clients of person-centered therapists sometimes need to adjust to the reality that their therapist will not guide, suggest, direct, or otherwise attempt to influence their decisions. Although this may create discomfort and uncertainty, clients of person-centered therapists often benefit ultimately by learning how to make choices and direct their lives. By doing so, they eventually become their own locus of evaluation and the authors of their lives. Most clients who find the person-centered therapist's nondirectiveness to be uncomfortable usually come to understand its purpose and adapt to it reasonably well. Person-centered therapy's effectiveness is, to a large degree, dependent on the client's inclination toward and capacity for self-reflection, something that can be cultivated to varying degrees in most clients.

Recently, a client of mine, a 26-year-old female doctoral student in a clinical psychology program, spontaneously addressed her experience with the nondirective structure of her therapy at the beginning of her 10th session. She stated:

> I want to comment on the therapy process itself, because this style of therapy or the way you do therapy, for me has been such a learning experience. And I think it's so effective for me, and so effective in general as well. I often think about how it's not structured, or the structure doesn't come from you. It comes from me and I just think it's really amazing. It has been amazing for me because I can see how I have to do all the work in a sense. I feel like I can't just come in here and sit, and then you sort of direct and guide and create the structure and I sort of fill in the blanks. Instead, I know that when I come in here that whatever is done in here will come from me. And so that has been so interesting because I think that it causes clients to work a lot more outside of sessions. And I just find that very powerful. And it's very difficult for me because I like structure and my barometer

sort of lies in the external, and so it's just been really scary, but in a good way, and it's just been very powerful for me. And I am just so impressed with this style of therapy. . . . I just find it interesting for me that it just so fits with what I need and I like that a lot. I think it's really challenging me and it's not comfortable yet but I'm OK with it. I think it's a "good" uncomfortable. And I just find myself working outside of session a lot because I know "OK, what am I going to bring on Monday." . . . I think it's been just really good for me and I really appreciate this therapy style itself and the way that you do it. So I just wanted to [share that]. (personal communication, 2009)

This insightful client, one who prefers structure in her life, has come to understand that the minimal structure and high level of freedom in person-centered therapy has its frustrations and rewards. Though somewhat ambivalent and uncomfortable initially about taking responsibility for how she uses therapy, she has noticed that she continues to reflect on her concerns and learning outside of the therapy session. Although person-centered therapy is challenging, it has resulted in her stretching herself. To her credit, this client has made great progress by fearlessly exploring sensitive aspects of herself and becoming accepting of heretofore-disowned aspects of herself.

In recent years, a number of experts in the field of psychotherapy (e.g., Bohart and Tallman, 1999) have come to realize that it is the client rather than the therapist who is the primary agent of constructive change.

When Rogers formulated his if-then hypothesis, it implied that if the *therapist* provided certain relational conditions, then the client would respond with constructive change. Although Rogers designated his approach as client/person-centered, his hypothesis placed most of the responsibility for creating the conditions for change on the therapist. In contrast, Bergin and Garfield's view (1994) suggests that clients' active participation and involvement in therapy are primarily responsible for their success. Further, research conducted by Michael Lambert (1992) suggests that 40% of the variance in outcome depends on client characteristics and resources. Clearly, clients don't change if they are passive or uninvolved participants; they need to take responsibility for their lives and make efforts to change.

BRIEF AND LONG-TERM STRATEGIES

A misconception about person-centered psychotherapy is that it is inevitably long-term therapy. It is not. Although it is not well known, most therapy is brief therapy. The modal number of sessions clients attend is *one* and most courses of psychotherapy are six sessions or less (Miller, Duncan, & Hubble, 1997). Similarly, the length of client-centered therapy varies from as few as 1 to more than 100 sessions, depending on the client's goals and severity of problems. I have seen many clients who have benefited from a single session, and the majority of clients make good progress in 10 sessions or less.

There is no fundamental alteration in the way client-centered therapy is practiced to achieve brevity. However, like other brief therapies, client-centered therapy may have a more limited focus, which results in the therapist and client agreeing to keep their attention and efforts on some circumscribed aspect of the client's problems.

A LONG COURSE OF THERAPY

Overview

Sabina is a single woman of African American descent in her late 40s with some college education who works for a law firm as an executive secretary. She has a 23-year-old son who lives with her on and off. Sabina's father left when she was 3 and died when she was 21. She had no contact with him after he left. Her son's father and she separated when her son, David, was 2. David's father has had minimal contact with him or Sabina since leaving. Her mother and sister live near each other and about 45 minutes away from Sabina.

I have seen Sabina in individual psychotherapy on a weekly, bi-weekly, or monthly basis for 3 years (with two breaks of about 6 months) and a total of 49 sessions to date. The concerns that brought her to therapy were persistent depression, anxiety attacks, unresolved conflicts with her mother and sister, and concerns about her son who has periodically spent brief periods of time in prison. Sabina has a number of health problems, including asthma, arthritis, recurring abdominal pain of unknown origin, and difficulty sleeping. She takes medication for depression, anxiety, asthma, and severe cramps.

A major concern is her lifelong conflicted relationship with her mother. Sabina's mother, who is in her mid-70s, left her and her sister with an aunt when Sabina was 3, something that troubled Sabina deeply because she could not comprehend why her mother would leave her at such a young age. Coming to terms with her feelings of being abandoned has been a major focus of therapy. Sabina's relationship with her mother is further complicated by her belief that her mother favors her older sister, who is in her late 40s.

Sabina identified a number of goals during the course of her therapy. However, for the purposes of the therapeutic illustration here, I will focus only on the primary goals of her therapy, including: (a) coming to terms with her strained relationships with her mother and family; (b) improving her health; (c) becoming an entrepreneur/businesswoman and real estate owner; (d) improving her organizational skills; (e) developing a more satisfying social life; (f) learning to accept and deal with being alone and single; and (g) losing weight.

Sabina is a bright, personable, attractive, outgoing, open, and straight-forward woman with a ready smile and friendly demeanor. She is a client I always looked forward to seeing and who uses her therapy sessions very effectively.

Initial Phase of Therapy

First Session

In the first minute of the first session Sabina said, "My mother writes (me) nasty letters. She likes the other daughter but not me." She indicated that after nine nasty letters, "it really shut me down. She always feels that she has to tell us off. Instead of talking personally, she writes nasty letters." Sabina acknowledged that she felt hurt, angry, and immobilized and withdrew from contact for a while. She began seeing a psychiatrist for medication for depression and anxiety and, soon after, sought psychotherapy. As she focused on the story of her relationship with her mother, Sabina said that her mother left her to live with her aunt for most of her childhood and adolescence while her mother moved to another state. She then stated simply, "I was abandoned." Later she commented, "I don't think my mother approves of me and who I am."

When I inquired about what she hoped for in therapy, Sabina said she hoped to come to terms with the rift she believes her mother has caused and that her mother would take steps to repair their relationship. She then added that she didn't expect that to happen and she needed to "stay out of the path of abuse." When she did visit her mother, she coped by "keeping it shallow." Sabina mentioned that her mother wants her and her sister, who is a nurse, to pay her mother's rent and generally do whatever her mother wishes (e.g., take her shopping, give her money, clean her house, buy things for her), something Sabina resents because she feels that her mother rarely reciprocates such kindnesses.

After listening to Sabina's pained feelings of rejection and disapproval from her mother, I commented, "You've been a bad daughter" to which she responded, "I've been a very bad daughter." A little later I asked her what kept her in the relationship. She replied, "She's my mother. You only get one. I feel a duty to honor my mother," in part because of her Christian religious beliefs. In short, Sabina continues to contend with enormous ambivalence toward her mother, detesting her mother's criticism and lack of interest, yet still hoping her mother will accept and value her.

Later in the first session, as Sabina was talking further about her mother and the hurt she experienced, she began to pull the sweater she was wearing around her. I commented on this seeming symbolic behavior, "You need to protect yourself," and she replied, "It's not safe." Sabina was attempting to cope with her pained relationship with her mother and her depression by sleeping up to 17 hours a day. She added, "I'm not living. I'm sleeping my life away." She did, however, go to work daily and functioned well in her job. Her life consisted mostly of working and sleeping to withdraw from her unhappy world.

Sabina mentioned that she had an on-and-off relationship with a man who was "the first person I dated in 13 years." She hoped to marry some day but was frustrated with the men she met over the years, including this relationship, and tended to avoid relationships. At the end of our first session I asked what, if anything, she might take from our first meeting. Sabina replied, "I need to look at my days and plan things and regulate my sleep." As I reflected on our first session, I was aware of liking Sabina, finding her endearing and appreciating her courage in being so vulnerable in sharing her pain and frustration. I felt compassion for her and hoped that she could come to terms with her despair about her relationship with her mother and get her life on track. Sabina's motivation to improve her life was evident. I had a sense that there was a resilient woman residing in the wounded soul I had met. By the session's end I had a good "feel" for who Sabina was and had a sense that she felt heard and supported. I was optimistic that the resilience I sensed in her would prevail.

First Few Months

In the next few weeks, Sabina continued to sleep a lot, remained withdrawn and isolated, and felt little motivation to do anything. Sabina readily engaged herself in therapy and was an open and active participant in our sessions. She began to see her excessive sleeping as a "cop-out" and began instead to use time spent in bed as a reward for doing something constructive. The focus of our sessions frequently returned to her mother, with whom she continued to have a great deal of "unfinished business." Sabina has never felt securely attached to her mother. During one session when she focused on her troubled relationship with her mother, I offered her the possibility of doing some gestalt empty-chair work in which she would alternately express herself to her mother and then respond back as she imagined her mother would. Sabina welcomed this opportunity and used it effectively, expressing her frustration and hurt that her mother rejected her son, favored her sister, doesn't tell the truth, and could be mean. The exercise seemed to empower her as she stood up to her mother.

The reader may wonder why a person-centered therapist is using techniques from gestalt therapy. In my view of what it means to be *client-centered*, the therapist brings forward for the client's consideration anything that may be of value in the current context. Because dealing with ongoing conflicts with her mother was a major issue for Sabina, it made sense to offer a method that would help her do so.

An issue that arose periodically was Sabina's belief that her mother preferred her older sister to her. In this regard we began to explore whether Sabina's self-esteem was dependent on whether her mother favored her sister. To a degree it was, though Sabina was aware that she had other sources of esteem in her life, especially work where she performed at a very high level.

By the end of the first 3 months of therapy, Sabina was getting out of bed earlier, doing more, exercising regularly, and functioning pretty well from day to day. She had begun visiting her mother periodically and calling more often as well. She reported that her visits were pleasant and without incident for the most part. We also spent more time examining the continuing effects of her mother's leaving her and her sister with Sabina's aunt in New Jersey as her mother went to live in New York. Sabina began to understand that, as a young adult, her mother was more intent on having a good time in her life than being a mother. This understanding was complicated by the fact that her mother would not acknowledge any failings, nor would she apologize for her disinterest and neglect.

I believe that in the early phase of our therapy, Sabina was aware that I "saw" her, liked her, and valued the person she was. I think she began to see herself a bit more through my eyes and to incorporate a more positive view of herself. She was also beginning to consider that her value was not lessened even if her mother preferred her sister to her.

Second Phase of Therapy

After attending therapy inconsistently for a few months, Sabina returned and resumed weekly sessions for the next 9 months. During this period Sabina broke up with her on-and-off boyfriend, bought an investment home in another state, and received a good performance review at work. Unfortunately, she badly hurt her knee in a fall. Regarding her investment purchase, she described herself as a "businesswoman" with pride. She said things had calmed down with her mother for the time being.

In addition to the central issues regarding her relationship with her mother, we continued to work on other important challenges in Sabina's life, including her anxiety about her son and his problems with the law, her relationships with men, and continuing health and weight problems. We made headway on all of these concerns. For example, regarding her son, Sabina had constantly been concerned about his getting his life on track but realized that his decisions, for better or worse, were beyond her influence most of the time and that there was a limit as to what she could do to help him. Regarding her issues surrounding weight, we discussed a strategy for her to "eat naturally" and attune herself more carefully to her body's wants and needs and eating accordingly.

We looked at other issues as well, including Sabina's difficulty in getting organized, conflicts with friends over money she had loaned them, and her philosophy of life. Over the course of the second phase of therapy, Sabina began to organize her priorities with to-do lists, practiced being more assertive with friends to whom she had given money, and developed a different focus toward life that she articulated as "the world is not mine to save." By practicing these skills and developing a simple philosophy of patience and perseverance, Sabina continued toward her goals in spite of personal setbacks and physical problems. I admired her resilience, determination, and hard-won progress.

Signs of Progress and Ongoing Conflicts

After a year of therapy, Sabina was showing considerable signs of progress. She became more assertive with her mother and no longer tolerated her mother's demeaning or critical remarks. She was sorting out her relationship with her mother and setting clearer boundaries. She was also becoming more proactive in managing her daily life and commented, "action beats depression." About a month earlier she had decided to discontinue her depression meds and seemed to have done so with no ill effects. She exercised (mostly walking) on a daily basis, benefited from being outside, felt better physically, and made progress losing weight. Her sessions began to focus more on who she was and who she wanted to be. Sabina's self-concept included a view of herself as a businesswoman and as a land investor.

However, as expected, there continued to be difficult contacts with her mother and periodic reemergence of her feelings that her sister was favored by her mother and that her sister wasn't very invested in her. As we continued to process Sabina's unhealed wounds resulting from her mother's leaving her as a young child, I began to understand her core family narrative and its continuing damage. During one session when we were discussing her mother leaving her, I offered to share my view of the larger picture that had emerged to see if it fit her experience. Sabina was receptive to hearing how this came together in my mind. My construction of the story was as follows:

> When you were a small child, your mother left to go live in New York to make a new life, leaving you and your sister to stay with your aunt. As a young child you could not understand how your mother could leave you. You were left feeling, "Why didn't she want to be with me?" "Don't I matter to her?" "How could she say she loves me and move away for all those years?" "There must be something wrong with me if my own mother doesn't want to be with me." In African American culture the mother is almost always the one who takes care of her "babies" because dads are often not around. But your mother decided she wanted to have an adventurous life more than she wanted to be a mother. Even today she still seems much more invested in herself than in you. And it still hurts you to see that she makes little effort to be with you. You missed out as a child and, today, you are still missing out on having her be your mother.

Sabina found this encapsulated summary to be both clarifying and painful since it accurately captured the lifelong complexity of hurt, anger, rejection, abandonment, ambivalence, regret, and loss associated with her mother. Her wound was slow to heal, in part because her mother was reluctant to discuss or acknowledge what effects her behavior had on Sabina. On the few occasions her mother did, she usually denied any wrongdoing or said she couldn't remember what she did. Sabina continued to visit her mother periodically but indicated that their contact was "superficial." There was "no personal sharing," "no depth" in their conversation, and "no warmth" and "no coldness." She felt frustrated that her mother's attitude was "I don't want to deal with this and I don't have to." Her mother's reluctance to take responsibility for her part in their strained relationship made it more difficult for Sabina to come to terms with it. Sabina's relationship with her mother was further complicated by her mother's fear of her son David and general unwillingness to be in his presence. Consequently, attempts to resolve her lifelong conflict with her mother resulted in her feeling abandoned again and reopened feelings that there was something wrong with her.

One recollection about her relationship was particularly telling: As an adolescent, Sabina made a long bus trip to see her mother. When she arrived, she was told by her mother to go back to her aunt's house because her mother had a date that evening and didn't want her date to know she had an adolescent daughter because it would reveal that she was older than she looked.

Sabina continued to hope that her mother would be more accepting and kindly toward her. She came to a familiar conclusion, saying, "I realize that my mother is mean." Generally, she coped with her conflicted relationship with her mother by limiting contact and by keeping their relationship superficial, a strategy that worked for both, though imperfectly. We agreed that her primary challenge was to decide what kind of relationship she could have with her mother that would not be damaging to her mental health.

Sabina did gradually learn what she could expect from her mother and what kind of relationship she could have with her. After undergoing knee surgery that left her in need of care, her mother came to spend 5 days with her and looked after her. Sabina commented that "she was well behaved." They had some discussions about their relationship during this time and Sabina was gratified that her mother finally admitted that she had written and said "horrible things" to her. Sabina felt that she had made a step forward in resolving her unfinished business with her mother and felt proud of herself for mustering her courage to confront her mother once again with her troubled feelings.

Sabina learned to limit her contact with her mother, sometimes for months at a time, when she determined that her mental health was better served by doing so. For a while this decision came with some guilt, but that guilt gradually diminished. She also came to realize, though painfully, that she could not depend on her family to be there for her. She commented, "I'm on my own and cannot depend on my family to support me."

Another source of progress for Sabina was her conflicted relationship with her older sister. As mentioned earlier, Sabina felt hurt by her mother's favoritism for her older sister. Eventually, Sabina mustered the courage to address this felt favoritism with her sister. The conversations proved to be fruitful, eased the slight she felt, and allowed her to be on better terms with her sister.

Third Phase of Therapy

Sabina changed her health insurance to a different provider, resulting in a gap of about 6 months in her therapy. However, I did see her once during this time before she began attending regularly again several months later. When she resumed therapy, it was clear that she had continued to work on her issues and that she was progressing. She had continued to learn more about herself, take responsibility for her life, and make increasingly better choices.

One major decision was to take care of herself *first* when she needed to by deciding how much contact and under what circumstances she would have contact with persons who were stressful for her. While she remained thoughtful of others, Sabina felt less guilty about establishing clearer and more acceptable boundaries with her mother, sister, other family members, and friends. At one point, she had not visited her mother for about 2 months. While she felt some mild guilt about this, she had decided that she needed to attend to her own mental and physical health more than being a dutiful daughter

An entire session had a theme of "I'm on my own," a bittersweet realization and acceptance that she cannot depend on her family to support her and that she needed to be her own primary support system while also deriving support from long-term friends.

Sabina became more philosophical and accepting about her son's being in and out of jail or prison periodically, recognizing that he needed to learn how to manage his life while accepting that she had done the best she could in providing support and guidance for him.

Sabina became somewhat more disciplined and organized in managing her daily affairs and finances and keeping her house in order but still struggled in this area. She continued to eat better and exercise regularly and lost 12 pounds.

An important realization Sabina came to was that she had become too isolated, spending most of her time at work or at home. She began to yearn for some fun and adventure in her life and was determined to "get out in the world more." She was considering what adventures she would pursue and with whom. Most important, Sabina was proud of herself for coming so far and maintaining her progress. Her general mood was positive and she was not experiencing depression or anxiety.

Update and Current Status

Sabina resumed therapy after a 6-month absence, mostly because of financial limitations. She has completed 3 years of therapy and now attends sessions every 2 weeks. She seems to be in the final phase of her therapy. Having made remarkable progress, she is mostly building on what she has achieved. A few changes are especially notable. Probably most important is that she has learned to take good care of her physical and mental health. She has given up the notion that she needs to "act like someone else wants you to." Consequently, her value as a person is generated primarily from within and is no longer attached to her mother's or family members' expectations of conditions of worth.

In this regard, she is no longer intimidated by her mother, refuses requests from her that she finds unacceptable, and speaks her mind to her when she thinks it appropriate. Sabina commented that she is at peace with what she is willing to do, or refuse to do, for her mother and noted that her mother has "mellowed out beautifully."

Her son, now 24, recently returned from prison. Sabina decided that her son still needs a bond with her as well as her support, guidance, and some "constructive criticism" on occasion. She reports that her son is "doing well."

In other areas, Sabina is also doing quite well. In her work as an executive secretary, Sabina said she received exemplary work reviews and commented that she had a "great year." Sabina's mood and sense of well-being are generally good. She has been getting out more with friends and increasing her range of activities outside of her house, and she has become more receptive to meeting men. Regarding her health, Sabina has now lost 34 pounds and appears much fitter. Although she still suffers abdominal pain, she does not allow the pain to compromise the quality of her life. In assessing her current state, Sabina said, "Life is good."

Therapeutic Illustration

Included below are excerpts from a session that Sabina found gut-wrenchingly difficult, emotionally draining, and powerful. It proved to be a major step forward in her coming to terms with and liberating herself from the most troublesome aspects of her relationship with her mother and family. In the session, she addressed many of the core issues she wrestled with over 3 years of therapy. I have added some comments throughout the transcript. As you read the transcript, you may want to note the frequent exclamation marks that point to the many powerful feelings Sabina expressed and processed throughout the session. If any session could be called a signature session, this would be Sabina's. It was as if we encountered the storm together, with her leading the way while I accompanied and supported her courage in wrestling with her most challenging issues.

Note: Just prior to the following exchange, Sabina expressed her frustration and disappointment that her niece only seemed interested in visiting her when Sabina paid her to do some housework.

T: You don't feel that you can depend on them [family] to be interested in you.

C: Yeah. That's my family. If there's no use there, and there's [an attitude of] "what's in it for me," then . . .

T: In other words, there's not much altruism in your family.

C: No! I guess it's so weird because of my concept of what family should be is different.

T: There's a gap between your family and your ideal view of a family.

C: Gap!? Gap is too small of a word, doctor.

T: Chasm?

C: Thank you.

T: So the bigger the gap, the bigger the disappointment.

C: Um Hm. Yeah. And it's just like they band together and think it's OK. So, I realize I've been feeling better about not calling my mother. My heart just isn't in it. And I call her one night, . . . it was a reach-out call on my part. I was not feeling myself. I couldn't exactly put a grasp on it. I called [my mother] and we did the formalities and I said "You know, I'm not feeling myself," and then she goes, "We're all like that sometimes.

You need to go talk to God or you need to go talk to your therapist." And I felt what she was saying was "Don't tell me about it."

T: In other words you're hearing, "If you're needy and troubled, go find somebody else to cry on their shoulder, not mine."

C: Yeah! That's what I interpret it. And it could have been just me. Like I said, I wasn't feeling myself. Maybe I was more sensitive, and I haven't been calling her.

T: What you were hoping for was . . .

C: "Tell me how you feel. What's wrong?"

T: You wanted your mom to be sympathetic.

C: Yeah. [just ask] "What's wrong?"

T: Just show that you're there so I know you care and that you'll support me.

C: Yeah! And she basically told me about she's been dealing with pain and when she asked about me, I told her, "I don't feel right. I'm not exactly myself." And she basically told me, "Go away" and then she said, "Got to go. Bye." End of conversation.

T: So you felt abandoned, I imagine.

C: Rejected would be the word.

T: More rejected [and] pushed away.

C: Yeah, "You have a problem today and I don't care about it." You know what I mean.

T: "I don't care about it" feels like "I don't care about you." (C: Uh Huh.) So that hurts.

C: So that hurts! And um, it's just been like weird. The pain has just been just devastating.

Comment: Despite many disappointments in her mother, Sabina reaches out for support and feels stung about the lack of care and sympathy displayed by her mother. However, Sabina is beginning to accept that she cannot depend on her mother to be there for her.

A few minutes later, Sabina addresses the hurt she feels at being left out of her family and also the emerging reality that her hoped-for family will likely never be realized.

C: Yeah, I'm feeling that, the whole group of them [mother, sister, niece] they just have no sense of family whatsoever. I think that my mother sets the leading role and my sister is following and my niece is following, which leaves me up here isolated and cut off.

T: So as you see it, your mother sets the tone for being selfish.

C: Yeah. Before my mother came out here, my sister and I were much closer. Before my mother came out here, my sister occasionally would ride up to my house. Then my mother started saying I live so far [away]. The next thing I know is my sister starts saying I live so far away so she doesn't make the effort to come up. And that was not there before my mother moved out here and put all of that in her [sister's] mind. Now my sister mimics my mother and then my niece mimics my sister so my niece says "it's so far, it's so far." So now the three in unison say "It's so far. You live so far away and that's the reason we don't come and see you."

T: So you hear what seems to be a lame excuse. It's really not that far in your mind to come up here [a 45-minute drive] if they really wanted to. But you see a lack of interest and effort (C: Yeah), which leaves you feeling not very cared about.

C: Yeah. Um hm. And I had spoken to my sister about a month ago about when she's having something [e.g., family get-together] and not inviting me, and she basically said that, "Well, I don't really have anything. It just kind of comes together." And I said, "I would like to know about it so that I could see if maybe I could come," and she said yeah, she would do that. And then I'm talking to my mother, and my mother turns around and tells me that they went out to Red Lobster. My sister didn't call and say they were all going to Red Lobster. Then my niece tells me that the holiday weekend, which I specifically asked my sister was she doing anything and she said "no," that she didn't do anything that Monday but that Sunday like she cooked and had them over. And I was like thinking in my mind, "Didn't I just ask you about these things?" So I don't know. She thinks these things are so different, or she just doesn't want me to come and she just won't say she just doesn't want me to come.

T: So you end up feeling left out.

C: I feel left out.

T: But you're not sure what is going on in your sister's mind, [you feel] that she's not being straight with you?

C: Exactly! Yeah. Exactly. I feel that nobody talks. Nobody really tries to talk.

T: You're kind of left out of the circuit, aren't you?

C: Yeah, I feel like I'm left out. However, if there's something they think I can do for either one of them [mother or sister], you'll hear one of them voice it, either for theirselves or either for the other party. Nobody voices for me or my son. (Mentions how mother and sister ask her to pay for things for them and take her for granted) . . . If I'm coming down there for any meal, they usually make me, I can't say make, they usually ask me to bring one of the most expensive dishes, and I yell, "I'm not paying for the ham this time!" The meat dishes, you know what I mean? And I'll get there and she'll have her friends show up with nothing but their heads. And, then, that's a holiday where they can exploit me.

T: It seems that you've put your finger on a word that captures a lot of what you're feeling.

C: Exploitation.

T: Exploited.

C: Um hm.

T: You're here to serve us, but we're not here to look after you.

Commentary: As I track Sabina's view of her family, she seems to be increasingly clear and righteously indignant about how she is treated by them. She is angry about being exploited and appears to be reaching her limit for tolerating the exploitation. While it is painful to see her family as it is, this is a vital step toward her deciding what relationships she is willing and not willing to have with family members.

In the next few minutes (omitted), Sabina mentions asking her family to her house for Thanksgiving, partly as a test of their interest in seeing her.

C: . . . I don't expect them to show up, and I don't care whether they do or not.

T: I want to say back to you what you just said. (C: um hm). "I don't expect them to show up at my Thanksgiving and I don't care if they do or not."

C: I don't expect them to show up, and I don't care whether they do or not. (emphatically)

T: You just assumed that they wouldn't come.

C: (whispering) They've never showed up before.

T: "They don't show up for me" is what you feel. (C: Yeah.) I don't need any more of this.

C: I don't. It's absolutely ridiculous. Part of it is painful, but part of it is insanity.

Commentary: Sabina is expressing her sobering reality about her family. As she does so, her strength and resolve to protect herself from further disappointment are evident. In the exchange above, on one occasion, I said back exactly what Sabina said (i.e., "I don't expect them to show up at my Thanksgiving, and I don't care if they do or not"). I did so to heighten the emotion and personal relevance of this statement, which addresses her attempts to achieve perspective and liberate herself from the pain and disappointment frequently associated with her family.

T: Fine! (imitating client). Part of you would like them to want to come, and part of you would just as soon not have to deal with it.

C: BINGO! I think that was well said, Dr. Cain. The last time they were at my house, they were so ugly, I just remember.

T: So that leads to something like, "I don't need this."

C: (in soft voice) Nobody does.

T: If you don't want to be here, don't be here (C: Yes.), because I don't need you here in a bad mood.

C: Exactly! Exactly. But it goes all the way to I don't need to go down there for abuse either.

T: Yes. That makes sense for you. "If that's what I'm going to experience, why do I want to put myself in that situation?"

C: You know, when I get down there, over the course of years my mother has the flame of that I have to do something for her when I come down there . . . It started out as a torch. You know, "Oh, you never do anything for me and your sister does everything for me. When you came down here, you're going to wash the windows and do the refrigerator and dah dah dah dah dah dah." And you know it got to the point where I just said, "No!" She was like, "when you come down here, all we do is sit and talk and play games," and I said, "It's called visiting." I don't come down there to be the maid.

T: You're feeling exploited again. Your mother wants you down there to do something for her, and not just to enjoy your company.

C: Exactly. And also my mother, who has the most lopsided opinion of what is equal when it comes to me and my sister, wants to sit there and dictate and punish me because my sister does [help in some way]. No.

T: It doesn't seem fair.

C: No. "I don't care what Bella [sister] does for you. I really don't care what she does for you. You're dealing with me now." This is where I am and this is where, you know, there's a line there. That's fine. "She's [sister] a nurse, she gives me a bath" [comment of Sabina's mother about what Sabina's sister does for her]. Well you know what? I don't really deal with naked bodies. So, I'll help you wash your back and get your clothes on, but that's my extent [limit], I'm not going to give you a whole body bath.

T: You're saying, "I have some limitations."

C: I definitely have some limitations, yeah. And she's like. "Well, I'm your mother. You're supposed to be willing to do anything for me." I'm like, "no." Mother, anybody, I have limitations there.

T: So you're no longer buying into, "I'm your mother, you're supposed to . . ."

C: No! No. (emphatically).

T: You've drawn your own line.

C: Yes.

T: There's some things I'm not willing to do anymore.

C: Exactly.

T: And the main thing is, "I'm not willing to do anything that starts to feel like I'm being exploited."

C: Yes! And if I can think about what she wants me to do, and if she were to pass away tomorrow, would I hate myself because I didn't give her a body bath? No, I wouldn't hate myself for it. And it's OK to say "no." Big Point.

T: So, you're at some peace with this decision, I see.

C: Yes, I am at some peace with this decision . . .

Commentary: Here Sabina has engaged her courage to stand up to her mother and set clear boundaries. She is saying in effect, "I will not allow you to exploit me. There are limits to what I am willing to do for you. I will not be your maid, nor will I regret this decision, even if you died tomorrow." Perhaps most important, Sabina seems to be at peace with her position. A few minutes later Sabina takes a further step forward by acknowledging the emotional turmoil her family elicits and begins to realize that they will likely never be the family she hoped to have. Her weariness suggests that she is moving closer to disengaging from them. As I reread these passages, I was reminded how agonizing this session was for Sabina. As she looked fearlessly into the cold reality of her family, she experienced the excruciating anguish of her disappointment and profound loss.

Analysis and Reflections
on Sabina's Course of Psychotherapy

Sabina used therapy effectively to draw on her personal resources to make great progress in almost all of her goals. Her involvement and active participation in therapy were consistently high. She came prepared each session to address issues of concern and did so in a courageous manner, even when the problems she dealt with were emotionally draining. Sabina consistently took responsibility for herself in therapy and in her daily life. She never complained about her fate or took the role of a victim in her family. Nor did she ever attribute her problems to racial prejudice, though she was certainly aware of its existence in her world. Instead, she engaged her will and determination to improve herself and her life. Her health problems, and especially her pain, were often debilitating and slowed her progress at times. Yet, despite the many difficulties she faced, she retained her positive attitude that she could deal with her challenges and thrive in her life.

I shared in Sabina's pride in her enormous progress over the past 2 years. We often celebrated her progress over the course of our work together.

Looking through the lens of person-centered therapy, Sabina was certainly motivated to alleviate some major stressors in her life, particularly the ongoing strains and unfinished business with her mother and family. Regarding her mother, she strove to make sense of her mother's leaving her at a very young age to have an adventurous life. The empathic exploration process we engaged in helped her understand that her mother was not invested in being a mother and that this was not a reflection on Sabina's worth. Thus, Sabina came to see herself as worthy on her own merits despite her mother's frequent criticism and limited interest or affirmation. Her self-regard was developed from a number of sources. Sabina was a highly regarded executive secretary who consistently received positive work evaluations. She also became a successful businesswoman by buying property in another state. A number of long-term friends valued Sabina's steadfast friendship, kindness, generosity, and authenticity in speaking her mind.

Thus, Sabina's friends supported her in ways that her family did not. She was a good mother who continued to support and accept her son despite his problems with the law. Sabina also learned to be her own locus of evaluation. Independent of others, she was able to acknowledge her qualities and achievements while accepting her setbacks and limitations. She had a clear sense of herself and good self-esteem.

One of the primary ways Sabina mobilized herself to change was to set goals for herself. These ranged from a daily to-do list to projecting larger goals over the course of a year and beyond. While some of our work was focused on how goal achievement was impaired by Sabina, more often we worked toward her finding ways to stick to her goals. To her credit, she consistently returned to her goals and persisted in finding ways to achieve them.

As I look at my role in Sabina's progress, a few things seem relevant. What I did that seemed to make a difference was consistently be fully present and listen intently and with genuine interest to all that concerned Sabina. As I listened to many of the tapes of our sessions, I realized that I allowed her to do a lot of the talking. I did so because Sabina used the sessions as a meditation on her life and how she was currently managing it, while also discovering necessary correctives. By responding empathically, I helped heighten, clarify, and explore her realities and to find her own ways to address issues and move forward. It is my perception that Sabina felt heard and understood by me and that she courageously took in and explored whatever we addressed. In terms of Sabina's creating a more stable positive image, some contributions of mine come to mind. I believe that I served as a steadfast source of support, encouragement, and consistent optimism about her capacity to change. I think my genuine affection and liking for Sabina were evident to her, as was my acceptance for her as she was, something that reduced the conditions of worth she felt from her mother. In fact, I cannot recall ever feeling critical of her or even having moments of discord. This is extremely unusual in my experience, and I am somewhat amazed and puzzled by it. My sense of our therapy was that we just "clicked" early on and that the mutual liking and respect we experienced was always evident. I was myself and she was herself throughout our work. Sabina was the kind of person I could imagine as a good friend. I admired her as a mother and felt that she would make a fine partner in the right relationship. Although our relationship remained within appropriate professional boundaries, there was certainly an element of friendship in it. I always felt we were partners working together on her behalf.

There were additional aspects of our relationship that had a constructive effect on our therapeutic work. Whenever I met Sabina in the waiting room, she responded with a big smile and friendly greeting, no matter how troubled she may have been that day. She seemed genuinely happy to see me, and I was always happy to see her. Her friendly and positive presence with me elicited a similar response in me. An important point here is that the quality of relationship between therapist and client is not solely dependent on the therapist's provision of empathy, congruence, and positive regard, a conceptualization that suggests that what therapists ideally do "for" clients is a unidirectional endeavor. Rather, therapist and client affect each other and, together, cocreate a relationship. My natural liking for Sabina was certainly enhanced by her liking for me. Laughter was a frequent part of our meetings, as were sober moments of engaging with serious issues and troublesome feelings. Sabina said that she appreciated my wisdom, understanding, and laughter. The fact that Sabina had difficulties with a number of men in her life, starting with her father, who let her down or abandoned her, was certainly not lost on me. It helped me understand how important it was to be a trustworthy and constant presence in her life, someone who did not let her down.

On occasion, Sabina made some spontaneous comments about my manner of relating to her. During one session, Sabina commented, "You keep it real," which I believe had two meanings: (a) I focused unhesitatingly on what was most relevant, however difficult; and (b) Sabina found me honest, direct, and trustworthy. I would add that we both "kept it real" by being transparent to each other.

Finally, I will share a few thoughts on my being a white therapist working with an African American woman. From the beginning, I never had the sense that our racial differences were an issue. I also had worked with many African American women over parenting issues when I was a child clinical psychologist for 8 years, something that familiarized me with black culture. However, a little nagging voice in the back of my head said I might be making an erroneous assumption. Some experts in the field of culture and race in therapy insist that race is always an issue. So I decided to ask if my being white was an issue in any way for her. Sabina said that my being a white male was not an issue for her. While we were, of course, aware of our racial differences, I related to Sabina the person much more than to Sabina the black person. I certainly paid attention to racial issues that arose (e.g., Sabina's own frustration over finding a suitable black male partner), but our racial differences did not seem to play any major role in our work together. While such racial differences surely do come into play, I have come to believe that if, or to what degree, such issues matter, the client is the best guide about how such issues might be addressed.

5

Evaluation

Rogers was a pioneer in initiating and publishing research studies on the process and effectiveness of person-centered psychotherapy beginning in the early 1940s. This research tradition has continued and today, about 70 years later, there is a substantial body of research supporting the effectiveness of person-centered psychotherapy with a wide range of clients and problems of all age groups. In 1984, C. H. Patterson conducted a "review of reviews" of the extensive research on the effectiveness of the core conditions of person-centered therapy. Patterson concluded:

> Considering the obstacles to research on the relationship between therapist variables and therapy outcomes, the magnitude of the evidence is nothing short of amazing. There are few things in the field of psychology for which the evidence is so strong. The evidence for the necessity, if not the sufficiency, of the therapist conditions of accurate empathy, respect, or warmth, and therapeutic genuineness is incontrovertible. (1984, p. 435)

In a recent and comprehensive review of research in person-centered therapy, Bozarth, Zimring, and Tausch (2002) summarized their findings as follows:

> In short, psychotherapy outcome research supports the major tenets of CCT [client-centered therapy]. The therapeutic relationship and the client's resources are the crux of successful therapy and the foundation of CCT. It is also clear that Rogers' specific hypothesis of the necessary and sufficient conditions . . . has received much more empirical support than some of the equivocal reviews of the middle 1970s imply. Research has supported the theory that a congruent therapist's experience of empathic understanding of the client's frame of reference and experience of unconditional positive regard are related to positive outcome. (p. 179)

RESEARCH SUPPORTING CORE CONDITIONS

Research on the relationship between the therapist conditions of empathy, unconditional positive regard, and congruence and client outcome is generally positive. The evidence for each therapist condition is summarized below.

Empathy

In recent years, there has been a revival of interest in the constructive impact of therapist empathy (Bohart & Greenberg, 1997). Watson and colleagues (2002) reviewed the research on therapist empathy and found that: (1) research consistently demonstrates that therapist empathy is the most potent predictor of client progress in therapy and is an essential component of successful therapy in every therapeutic modality; (2) no study shows a negative relationship between empathy and outcome; (3) client ratings of therapist empathy are stronger predictors of successful outcome than the ratings of external judges or therapists; (4) strong behavioral correlates of empathy include (a) therapist direct eye contact and concerned expression, (b) a forward trunk lean and head nods, (c) a vocal tone that communicates interest and emotional involvement, (d) clarity of communication, and (e) use of emotional language; (5) conversely, therapist interruptions, advisement and reassurance, and a detached or mechanical vocal tone were negatively correlated with therapist empathy.

In a research review of 47 studies and 190 tests of the relationship between therapist empathy and outcome, Greenberg, Elliott, Watson, and Bohart (2001) reported that therapist empathy has a medium effect size that accounts for about 10% of outcome variance. A sobering piece of evidence is that lack of therapist understanding is consistently associated with negative outcomes (Mohr, 1995).

Sachse and Elliott's microprocess research (2002) showed that therapist empathic responses might deepen, maintain, or flatten client experiential processing and self-exploration. Further, they showed that clients do little experiential processing on their own and do not deepen their processing unless the therapist provides deepening empathic responses.

A recent qualitative study by Barbara Grote (2005) on the "experience of feeling really understood in psychotherapy" found that this experience involved clients' feeling (a) safe, (b) accepted, (c) relieved, (d) validated, (e) heard, (f) seen/known, (g) engaged with an active co-participant, (h) a sense of intimacy with the therapist, (i) surprised and experiencing a sense of awe at the discovery of a core truth or new way of looking at a situation, (j) more self-acceptance, and (k) engaged with a compassionate, genuine "other." In short, multiple attitudes, qualities, skills, and behaviors contribute to the client's sense of being heard and seen accurately, some of which differ from what most therapists conceive as empathic understanding. Similarly, Bachelor's research (1988) demonstrated that what clients perceive to be empathic varies from client to client and does not always correspond to what therapists consider an empathic response.

Both personal and therapeutic experience provides compelling evidence that feeling understood and accepted by important others is conducive to our well-being. Further, research on therapist "listening," a form or component of empathy, shows that it is rated highly by clients as helpful, especially when clients are struggling with suicidal impulses (Cooper, 2008). Conversely, Paulson, Everall, and Janice (2002) found that the therapist's failure to listen, as perceived by clients, was extremely unhelpful or hindering. Regardless of one's therapeutic approach, the desire to hear our clients, enter into their experiential worlds, and communicate that understanding is almost inevitably helpful and never harmful, while failure to do so has adverse effects.

Unconditional Positive Regard

Twenty-four relatively recent studies address therapists' "affirmation" of clients, a concept that includes acceptance, nonpossessive warmth, and unconditional positive regard. A large majority of the studies showed a positive correlation between affirmation and client outcomes, while some findings were neutral and only one was negative (Orlinsky, Grawe, & Parks, 1994). Combining the findings of Orlinsky, Grawe, and Park with studies from Orlinsky and Howard's earlier (1986) review, Farber and Lane (2002) note that the authors

> summarized the results of 154 findings . . . drawn from a total of 76 studies. They found that 56% of the findings were positive, and that, again, the findings based on the patients' . . . sense of the therapist's positive regard yielded even a higher rate of positive therapeutic outcomes, 65%. (p. 184)

In sum, 87 findings showed a statistically significant positive relationship between therapist affirmation and positive outcomes, 63 findings showed no relationship, and 4 showed a negative relationship. Thus, the research evidence for therapist unconditional positive regard is substantial. Further, while therapist unconditional positive regard may, at times, show no demonstrable effect on client outcome, it is rarely negatively related to outcome. Clinical observation and everyday experience suggest that most persons/clients find another's regard or affirmation to be supportive and therapeutic. Conversely, therapist responses that impair therapy include: boredom; rote and impersonal responses; lack of compassion, understanding, and respect; coldness or arrogance; and irritation or anger—all in clear contrast to acceptance and regard (Feifel & Eels, 1963; Glass & Arnkoff, 2000).

Congruence

The research on the impact of therapist congruence has been more ambiguous and contradictory. Of 77 results reviewed, only 34% showed a positive correlation with positive outcomes, while two thirds showed no correlation.

No negative relationships between therapist congruence and outcome were found. When clients rated their therapists, results were somewhat more positive (Klein, Kolden, Michels, & Chisholm-Stockard, 2002). These authors conclude that "there is both empirical and theoretical justification for congruence as a central component of a complex conception of the therapy process" (p. 396). Studies that ask clients to identify the most important aspects of their therapy in relationship to outcome find that therapist openness, realness, or genuineness are rarely cited (Burckell & Goldfried, 2006; Feifel & Eels, 1963). However, it is interesting to note that therapist trustworthiness does emerge as an important characteristic identified by clients in good outcomes (Burckell & Goldfried, 2006; Conte, Ratto, Clutz, & Karasu, 1995). It is likely that therapist trustworthiness lends credibility to therapist empathy and unconditional positive regard.

It is difficult to make sense of these inconsistent findings. Kirschenbaum (1979) believes, as I do, that congruence was the least clearly defined and understood of Rogers's core conditions. In sum, because congruence remains "the most difficult of the core conditions for therapists to get right" (Kirschenbaum & Jourdan, 2005, p. 43), conceptual clarity about the meaning of congruence is needed as well as research to understand better how and when congruence can be communicated therapeutically and without harm.

RESEARCH ON OTHER PERSON-CENTERED PSYCHOTHERAPIES

Focusing-Oriented Psychotherapy

Hendricks's review of the research (2002) shows that: (a) higher levels of experiencing in clients correlates with successful outcomes in a variety of therapeutic orientations and client problem types; (b) the ability to focus and increase experiencing level can be taught to clients; and (c) therapists who themselves focus seem to be more effective in enabling their clients to focus.

The client's personal construction of the meaning of events in therapy shows that experiencing is positively related to outcome in 51% of

39 studies (Orlinsky et al., 1994, as cited in Bergin & Garfield, 1994). Iberg (1996) found that clients reported greater impact in sessions when therapists used focusing-oriented questions. Leijssen (1996) conducted a study to determine whether focusing enhanced client-centered therapy. She found that 75% of positive sessions used focusing steps, while only 33% of negative sessions used focusing. Client focusing, whether a part of focusing-oriented psychotherapy or other person-centered therapies, seems to enhance the quality of individual sessions and good outcome.

Pre-Therapy

There is a modest and accumulating amount of research supporting pre-therapy (Dekeyser, Prouty, & Elliott, 2008). Outcome research conducted on a small sample of persons with schizophrenic symptoms or intellectual disability suggests that "average descriptive and controlled effect sizes for these studies are large, even though they lack statistical power" (Dekeyser et al., 2008, p. 51). There was additional evidence from three single case studies that "communicative contact can improve over a period of one to two years" and especially in the last phase of treatment (p. 51). While research is sparse, years of clinical experience suggests that pretherapy is quite effective with seriously impaired persons.

Emotionally Focused Psychotherapy (EFT)

Attention to client emotion is characteristic of all person-centered therapies, but it is the primary focus of EFT or process–experiential (PE) therapists. In the last 20 years, EFT has been extensively researched, led by Les Greenberg and Robert Elliott, the founders of this approach.

Research on depth of experiencing in therapy has been shown consistently to relate to good outcome. The literature on client processing of emotion reviewed by Greenberg, Korman, and Pavio (2002) concluded that: (a) processing information in an experiential manner is associated with productive client involvement and predicts successful outcome; (b) therapies focusing on clients' emotional experience, when successful, are associated with changes in clients' in-session emotional experiences; (c) emotion is important in reorganizing personal meaning; and (d) research on therapist processing of client emotion indicates that the individual's ability to accurately differentiate his or her emotional experience is integral to healthy functioning.

In a recent review of PE psychotherapy research, Elliott and Greenberg (2002) report that: (a) 11 studies yielded large pre-to-post therapy effect sizes with a mean effect size of 1.34; (b) two controlled studies showed a large advantage for PE clients versus wait-list control groups; and (c) in five comparative outcome studies, PE therapy was superior to group psychoeducational treatments, cognitive behavioral therapy, a cognitive restructuring treatment, behavioral problem solving, and client-centered therapy, for a variety of problems.

A randomized clinical trial that compared the effectiveness of EFT to client-centered therapy showed that both CCT and PE were effective treatments for alleviating depression although PE was more effective in alleviating interpersonal problems and increasing self-esteem (Greenberg & Watson, 2006). In a replication study, results demonstrated that with a second sample of 38 clients (19 in each group), EFT was more effective in alleviating depressive symptoms and equally as effective in alleviating interpersonal problems and increasing self-esteem. When the two samples were combined, providing sufficient power to find differences, EFT was found to be more effective on all indices of change (Goldman, Greenberg, & Angus, 2006).

Goldman, Greenberg, and Pos (2005) looked at the relationship between theme-related depth of experiencing and outcome in experiential therapy with depressed clients. Analyses revealed that client level of experiencing (EXP) on core themes in the last half of therapy was a significant predictor of reduced symptom distress and increased self-esteem. Studies that examined expressed arousal showed that a combination of visible emotional arousal and experiencing was a better predictor of outcome than either index alone, supporting the hypothesis that it is not only arousal of emotion but also reflection on aroused emotion that produces change (Missirlian, Toukmanian, Warwar, & Greenberg, 2005). A recent study showed that clients with better outcomes expressed significantly more productive highly aroused emotions than clients with poorer outcomes, suggesting that expression of highly aroused emotions is important in facilitating change (Greenberg, Auszra, & Hermann, 2007).

In an extensive review of the literature, Elliott, Greenberg, and Lietaer (2004) concluded that "experiential treatments have been found to be effective with depression, anxiety, and trauma, as well as to have possible physical health benefits and applicability to clients with severe problems, including schizophrenia" (p. 510). Regarding the effectiveness of PE/EFT for depression, Greenberg and Watson (2006) concluded:

> Client-centered and process experiential therapy . . . have been shown to be effective in alleviating depressive symptoms, with process experiential therapy showing greater effectiveness overall. Regardless of type of treatment, emotional arousal and depth of experiencing were found to predict outcome. (p. 15)

Emotion-Focused Therapy for Couples

In a meta-analysis on EFT for couples, an effect size of 1.3 was found (Johnson, Hunsley, Greenberg, & Schindler, 1999). Approximately 90% of treated couples rated themselves better than controls while 70–73% of couples recovered from marital distress at follow-up. The Society for Clinical Psychology of the American Psychological Association has identified emotionally focused couples therapy as an empirically supported treatment for marital distress. EFT for couples "is empirically validated on several levels: on the level of treatment outcome, and on the levels of the relational theory in which it is based and key moments and factors in the change process" (Johnson, 2007, p. 47).

In sum, there is a large and growing body of research demonstrating the effectiveness of EFT for depression, anxiety, trauma, and marital issues, with some evidence of benefits for health problems. Of all of the person-centered psychotherapies, EFT has clearly received the most empirical support in the last 10 years.

SPECIFIC PROBLEMS AND CLIENT POPULATIONS WHERE PERSON-CENTERED THERAPY IS AND IS NOT EFFECTIVE

Research support for client-centered therapy exists in the following groups and problem types (a) anxiety disorders, including panic, agoraphobia, and generalized anxiety; (b) depression; (c) relational problems; (d) high functioning schizophrenics; (e) psychosomatic problems; (f) juvenile delinquents;, (g) psychiatric inpatients; (h) college students; (i) teachers; (j) children; (k) elders; (l) persons with cancer; (m) borderline personality disorder; (n) shyness; and (o) positive changes in self-concept (Bozarth, Zimring, & Tausch, 2002; Elliott, Greenberg, & Lietaer, 2004; Greenberg, Elliott, & Lietaer, 1994; Rogers, 1961; Truax & Carkhuff, 1967; Truax & Mitchell, 1971). In sum, the research evidence of the last 40 to 65 years indicates that person-centered therapy is indeed effective for the most prevalent problems for which people seek therapy.

Most systems of psychotherapy have a bias that their approach is effective with all forms of psychopathology. When research is reported by scientists with an allegiance for the therapeutic approach being reported, the success rates trend to be skewed in a positive direction. Thus, one must assess critically the allegiance factor when claims of therapeutic success seem particularly high.

While the evidence suggests that most major therapeutic approaches are roughly equivalent in effectiveness with the most common forms of psychopathology (e.g., depression, anxiety, interpersonal problems), all have their limitations. This is certainly true of person-centered therapy. When Rogers assessed the effectiveness of his approach at various points in time, he acknowledged some likely limitations. In *Counseling and Psychotherapy* (1942), Rogers addressed the possible limitations of nondirective psychotherapy. He made the following comment:

> The approach of the non-directive group applies to the overwhelming majority of clients who have the capacity to achieve reasonably adequate

solutions for their problems. Counseling, from this viewpoint, cannot be
the only method for dealing with that small group—the psychotic, the
[mentally] defective, and perhaps others—who have not the capacity
to solve their own difficulties, even with help. (p. 128)

About 10 years later in *Client-Centered Psychotherapy* (1951), Rogers
acknowledged that "it seems to have been true that counselors have been
less successful with those individuals who are aggressively dependent, who
insist that the counselor shall take responsibility for the cure" (p. 189).

In the late 1950s, Rogers and his colleagues began a challenging
research project to assess the effectiveness of client-centered therapy with
schizophrenic persons. This research with hospitalized schizophrenic
persons, reported in *The Therapeutic Relationship and Its Impact* (Rogers,
1967), showed only modest results at best. Rogers himself acknowledged
that person-centered therapy may not be effective with persons who
showed little motivation to change and who made little effort to engage
in therapy. The amotivational effects of schizophrenia make it a challenge for therapies that rely on the client's natural tendency to actualize his or her potential. Speaking of "chronically psychotic individuals"
whose socioeconomic status was generally low, Rogers and Stevens (1967)
acknowledged that

we are probably dealing with one of the most difficult groups ever
worked with, in terms of the probability of change . . . we are dealing
with individuals who are not consciously desirous of psychotherapy,
who tend to have the view that "talking can't help," and who do not
see the therapist as a potentially helpful person. (p. 185)

Consequently, Rogers and his colleagues learned that they needed to
modify their typical therapeutic response style since empathic responding in the traditional fashion did not engage schizophrenic persons in a
therapeutic process. Therapists learned that they needed to be more active
and creative in finding ways to make effective contact with clients whose
impairment often took the form of social withdrawal.

During the schizophrenic research project, Rogers and his colleagues also worked with a "normal" population of low socioeconomic status that Rogers described as unmotivated since this group was not actively seeking psychotherapy. Rogers made a telling observation that there was a "general lack of success in trying to form a facilitative relationship with unmotivated 'normals' of low socio-economic status" (1967, p. 186). I believe this observation, certainly consistent with clinical experience, has implications for altering Rogers's theory of psychotherapy. Where initially he believed that it was sufficient for the client to be anxious or in a state of incongruence for therapy to take place, he now began to understand the critical importance of client motivation for therapeutic help if therapy was to occur, regardless of whether the clients were "normal" or severely impaired.

Person-centered therapy, even optimally practiced, is not an ideal fit for all clients. For some clients, the therapist's nondirectiveness regarding content and structure of therapy is problematic. Some clients experience the person-centered therapist as uninvolved and too passive, as someone who listens without offering much in the way of direction, guidance, or specific technique. Some clients inquire, during the first phone contact when they are seeking a therapist, if the therapist will do more than "just listen." This concern usually comes from a client whose therapist seemed be a passive listener who didn't seem to be actively engaged and responsive. In short, it seems that while most clients thrive on the freedom provided by person-centered therapy, a minority find it problematic and prefer more direction and structure.

Some forms of psychopathology simply respond better to other therapeutic approaches than person-centered ones. Obsessive-compulsive disorder responds well to exposure and response prevention, while phobias respond well to systematic desensitization and exposure. Persons with psychological disorders with a primary or strong biological component such as autism, severe and chronic schizophrenic disorders, panic disorder, pain disorders, severe mental retardation, and Tourette's disorder are probably not ideally suited to person-centered therapy.

PERSON-CENTERED THERAPY
WITH DIVERSE CLIENTS

Each person is in some respect
like every other person,
like some other person,
and in some ways like no other person.

—Kluckholm & Murray, 1959, p. 53

As early as the 1950s client-centered therapy was addressing issues of culture and diversity. Eugene Gendlin (1986) recalls that Rogers and his colleagues at the University of Chicago Counseling Center led the way in demonstrating respect for clients from diverse backgrounds and experiences, noting that "The counseling center was the only place where a black person or a gay person could get therapy without all of the nonsense around it." Rogers trained the counseling center staff to approach each individual in an open-minded way until the client disclosed his or her issues of concern. When race or culture or any form of diversity was an issue for the client, then those aspects of the person's life became an essential part of therapy. The desire and goal of the client-centered therapist was to hear, comprehend, and respond in a receptive and accepting manner to whatever aspects of that person's life and sociocultural context were relevant. It was understood that all clients of diverse experiences would inform receptive and inquiring therapists about their worlds when such differences became relevant.

Person-centered therapy is naturally suited to clients in a diverse world because it places a high priority on understanding each unique individual in the broader context of his or her life. Person-centered therapists readily look at all of the variables that are of personal import to clients and focus on whatever aspects of clients' lives that are most relevant in their daily functioning.

Colin Lago, one of the leading person-centered authorities on culture and diversity, makes a strong case that persons from minority groups experience disproportionate discrimination and oppression from the majority society. He points out that persons from the dominant culture have a privileged status and that difference and diversity are usually defined by the majority culture. He comments:

> Counseling across difference and diversity demands that therapists
> enhance their awareness of their own identity development and atti-
> tudinal base as well as developing their knowledge of the specific
> minority client groups with whom they work [including] . . . the
> myriad of discriminatory mechanisms that pervade society . . . and
> [with] a commitment and willingness to seek new language(s) and
> behaviors that are respectful and anti-discriminatory for all clients.
> (Cooper et al., 2007, p. 252)

Therapists' embedded beliefs, attitudes, and behaviors can be so ingrained that they often become unquestioned aspects of their identity. The "self" of the therapist always has a societal context that provides the lens through which he or she views others who are unlike him or her, including the therapist's prejudices and stereotypes. While we are in some ways like all others or some others, we cannot assume that the belief system embedded in person-centered theory and philosophy is a good fit for persons who are substantially unlike us in some ways. Ongoing self-scrutiny is especially critical if the therapist is a member of the dominant culture, which is the case for the large majority of person-centered therapists in the United States. Similarly, therapists from minority cultures or groups also need to raise their awareness of how their identities as minorities and experiences of being different influence their therapeutic behavior.

Person-centered therapy offers a potent approach to working with persons with a wide range of cultural and diverse experiences. The core therapist conditions of empathy, unconditional positive regard, and congruence are qualities that are universal or near universal in that they are likely to have a constructive impact on all clients, regardless of culture or a variety of differences from the hypothetical "mainstream." Compatible with this position, Sue and Sue (1990) agree that "qualities such as respect and acceptance of the individual, unconditional positive regard, understanding the problem from the individual's perspective, allowing the client to explore his or her own values, and arriving at an individual solution are core qualities that may transcend culture" (p. 187).

Ideally, person-centered therapists enter each session with a new client with an awareness that there is no one on earth like *this* client. Although a specific client shares at least some aspects of his or her experiences with other persons who share his or her race, gender, cultural background, age, and other attributes, person-centered therapists consciously attempt to lay aside any preconceptions or predispositions they may have about their clients. A fundamental question person-centered therapists bring to therapy is *"What is it like to be you?"* including any and all aspects of one's life that matter in some meaningful and impactful way. Although person-centered therapists are aware of obvious diversity factors (e.g., race, gender, disability), they initially make no assumptions about the relative importance of those factors to the client before them. They expect that each therapeutic journey will be unique and tailored to address the diversity issues that are relevant to each client.

I have long argued (Cain, 1989, 1990) that the classical form of person-centered therapy needs to be adapted when it does not ideally fit the needs of the unique person sitting before the therapist. I believe this can be accomplished while retaining the core values and premises of the approach. Some modifications of assumptions may be desirable to expand the approach's range of effectiveness with clients from other cultures. Sue and Sue (2003) have identified three competencies of the culturally skilled counselor. I believe these guidelines are also applicable for diversity in clients that extends beyond culture (e.g., sexual orientation, handicap). I will address each competency in terms of how well person-centered therapy meets each criterion for diversity and suggest possible modifications as appropriate.

Competency 1: Self-Awareness of One's Own Assumptions, Values, and Biases

As mentioned earlier, it is incumbent on person-centered therapists to raise their consciousness about the assumptions they hold and constantly assess their effects on clients, especially clients sufficiently different from them in some meaningful way. By the early 1950s, Rogers encouraged therapists to be aware of their own assumptions and values. One of Rogers's colleagues, Nicholas Hobbs (1951), stated:

> One of the cardinal principles in client-centered therapy is that the individual must be helped to work out his own value system, with a

> minimal imposition of the value system of the therapist. . . . This
> value, which affirms the individual's right to choose his own values,
> is believed to be therapeutically helpful. (p. 292)

Rogers took the position (1977) that clients deserve a "respectful hearing" of all attitudes and feelings, no matter how "extreme" or "unrealistic" (p. 113). To the degree that person-centered therapists embrace these sentiments, they are likely to reassess periodically their own values and assumptions and to make appropriate accommodations in the way they respond to the unique values and needs of clients' individual differences. The person-centered approach has been criticized for reflecting Rogers's and many Americans' values of independence, individualism, and self-determination. This position may conflict with persons who embrace collectivist views or who are strongly influenced by family values and expectations. To work effectively with such individuals, person-centered therapists would do well to suspend or set aside their own values and be receptive to the powerful influence and merits of their clients' family structure and values and culture. For example, in Deaf culture enormous pressure is often exerted on deaf children (and later on adults) to embrace sign language as opposed to spoken language. While this stance may run counter to the values of a hearing person-centered therapist, an understanding of this strongly held position and subsequent modifications in the therapist's assumptions about it are appropriate and desirable.

Competency 2: Understanding the Worldview of the Culturally Different Client

All therapists would serve their clients by learning as much as possible about the worldviews of their clients, whether cultural, those that emerge as a result of the client's experience (e.g., sexual orientation, poverty), or those that result from the client's need to cope with a difficult condition (e.g., blindness). The sensitive person-centered therapist would seek to understand what it is like to live as a gay, quadriplegic, or low-income person while refraining from stereotyped views and instead recognizing that persons within a subgroup have diverse experiences and attitudes. Rogers

(1951) believed that "the only way to understand another culture is to assume the frame of reference of that culture" (p. 494). MacDougall (2002) commented that Rogers "promoted counselor acquisition of knowledge of clients in their cultural settings, knowledge of cultural anthropology or sociology with actual experiences of living with or dealing with culturally diverse clients" (p. 52).

Competency 3: Developing Appropriate Intervention Strategies and Techniques

In *The Necessary and Sufficient Conditions for Therapeutic Personality Change*, Rogers (1957) did not specify how the therapist qualities of empathy, unconditional positive regard, and congruence might be implemented in the therapeutic process. His theory allowed for variations in how such universal qualities might be provided. Therefore, modifications in therapeutic style are acceptable, desirable, and sometimes necessary to meet the needs of a particular client.

One way in which person-centered therapy might be modified to meet the needs of diverse populations is to assess whether therapist nondirectiveness has a facilitative or impairing effect on diverse clients. Although nondirective attitudes and behavior on the part of the client-centered therapist may be experienced as freeing the client, they may have the opposite effect. As mentioned earlier, rigid insistence on nondirectiveness for all clients, regardless of culture, personal preference, learning style or other forms of diverse experience, may be experienced as an imposition that does not fit the client's interpersonal and therapeutic learning needs. MacDougall (2002) has argued that "to be truly person-centered, counselors need to allow themselves to be more directive if the culture(s)/circumstances of the client warrant it" (p. 54).

The optimal form of client-centered therapy would be "client-informed" or "client-directed," which suggests that the client plays a strong and collaborative role in how the therapy is implemented. In this approach, the therapist is sensitive to all of the variables that influence the client's life, including cultural and other forms of diversity. Finally, person-centered therapists need to consider carefully the possibility that this approach may not be sufficient in and of itself and be willing to offer any and all personal and professional resources that may be of therapeutic value, including concepts and methods from other approaches.

OBSTACLES OR PROBLEMS USING PERSON-CENTERED THERAPY WITH DIVERSE CLIENTS

Every system of psychotherapy has limitations and areas where some sacred cows are not examined critically. For person-centered therapy, belief in an *actualizing tendency* is the bedrock concept upon which the approach is built; thus, it deserves critical analysis.

Person-centered therapists take as a given that the individual has a natural tendency toward growth and healthy functioning. Because that tendency is believed to be present in every client, person-centered therapists assume that if the core conditions are provided to a sufficient degree, the actualization tendency will enable clients to tap their resources for constructive growth. However, for some clients in our increasingly diverse world, self-actualization and autonomy do not represent their highest values or optimal goals. Persons from collectivistic cultures are oriented less toward self-actualization and more toward intimacy, connection, and harmony with others and toward what is best for the community and the common good. Self-actualization is a value that is embraced by mainstream North Americans who are encouraged to "be all you can be" and are told that "you can be whatever you want to be." Some have criticized this position as one of self-absorption, ethno-centrism, and egoism. In today's culture in the United States, there is considerable evidence that celebrating the self is a frequent endeavor, especially in younger generations (e.g., Twenge, 2006). In contrast, Alfred Adler believed that "social interest," a genuine concern and caring for others, represented the highest level of psychosocial development. Similarly, Maurice Friedman (1992) has suggested that self-actualization occurs as a byproduct of a confirming dialogue with another person and suggests that valuing actualization of the self may result in losing sight of or a diminished valuing of others.

Research (e.g., Greenberg et al., 2002) clearly shows that helping clients process their emotional experiences is related to good outcome. However, it is also true that engaging clients' emotion requires considerable sensitivity and relational skill on the part of the therapist since experiencing problematic emotion is often arduous, painful, threatening, and disturbing for many clients. In many cultures emotional expression is minimized, sometimes suppressed, and even unacceptable in some situations. Therefore, person-centered therapists need to be cognizant of these cultural variations and modify the ways they respond to client emotion.

As mentioned previously, the manner in which the therapist's empathy, congruence, and unconditional positive regard are communicated may need to be modified to fit the needs of a wide variety of persons and cultures. For example, a therapist's direct expression of empathy might result in a client feeling exposed and vulnerable. Some clients may experience powerful empathic expression as a violation of the distance they prefer in the therapy relationship. Similarly, strong expressions of congruence or positive regard on the therapist's part may be intimidating to clients who are not prepared for such powerful and intimate relating.

As you will recall, Rogers created nondirective psychotherapy in the 1940s because he believed the therapies available at that time tended to be too "therapist-centered" and did not trust the resourcefulness of the client. Some clients, particularly from certain cultural groups, may prefer a more directive therapy since they view the therapist as the "doctor" or expert. Further, therapist nondirectiveness may also be too constricting for the therapist and client. That is, rigid insistence on nondirectiveness for all clients, regardless of culture, personal preference, learning style, or other forms of diversity may be experienced as an imposition that does not fit the client's interpersonal and therapeutic learning needs. Thus, the belief that nondirective attitudes and behavior are essential for all clients deserves further critical attention. Research (e.g., Beutler & Clarkin, 1990) shows that some clients do better with more directive therapists, while others do better with nondirective therapists.

144

6

Future Developments

Person-centered therapy remains a work in progress. It has limitations and imperfections, as do all models of psychotherapy. Carl Rogers always took the position that his necessary and sufficient conditions statement was a hypothesis subject to revision and that person-centered therapy should continue to evolve and change, especially in light of new research evidence. On occasion, he acknowledged sincere doubt about the person-centered approach, feeling a great burden of responsibility about whether the ideas he advanced were flawed and whether he might be misleading people (Kirschenbaum, 2007). Believing that "the facts are friendly" even if they suggest alterations to the current approach, Rogers supported such developments. In 1986, a year before he died, he commented: "The approach is paradoxical. It emphasizes shared values, yet encourages uniqueness. . . . it encourages those who incorporate these values to develop their own special and unique ways of being, their own ways of implementing this philosophy" (Rogers, 1986, pp. 4–5). Rogers was not only receptive to modifications in theory and practice but urged others to pursue such advances. At this point I will provide a critical analysis of Rogers's necessary and sufficient conditions formula, followed by a proposal for optimal conditions for therapy that draws from the various person-centered therapies, research evidence, theory, and clinical experience.

CRITICAL ANALYSIS AND MODIFICATIONS IN ROGERS'S NECESSARY AND SUFFICIENT CONDITIONS HYPOTHESIS

Surprisingly, Rogers's hypothesis has remained unmodified since he first published it in 1957, even though Rogers himself expected it to be altered in the light of new research and clinical evidence. However, in order to advance theory and practice, we need to review critically Rogers's hypothesis with an eye toward assessment of its contributions, strengths, limitations, and need for refinement and expansion.

When Rogers first published this seminal paper more than 50 years ago, psychotherapy research was still in its beginning stages. Psychoanalysis and its offshoots were the dominant voices in theory and practice, behavior therapy was just beginning to arrive on the scene, and cognitive therapies had not yet emerged. There were only a few dozen approaches to therapy, no theories of psychotherapy texts, and relatively few groundbreaking psychotherapy texts. The available body of psychotherapy research was sparse and research methodology was unsophisticated. Rubinstein and Parloff published the first major text summarizing psychotherapy research in 1958. However, since 1957, an enormous body of increasingly sophisticated research in the field of psychotherapy has been conducted that has generated substantial advancement in how all major theories of psychotherapy are conceived and practiced. Yet, relatively little of this research influenced Rogers or other person-centered scholars to modify Rogers's theory or practice in any substantial way until the last few decades.

The first question that arises is whether the six conditions proposed by Rogers are both necessary and sufficient for therapeutic personality change. Many psychotherapy theorists and practitioners have doubted for quite some time that these conditions are necessary *and* sufficient for all kinds of clients and problems. Rogers's biographer of 30 years, Howard

Kirschenbaum, summarized the contemporary evaluations of Rogers's hypothesis as follows:

> In spite of all the research support for empathy, positive regard and congruence, even some strong advocates of client-centered/ experiential therapy have conceded or concluded that the core conditions may neither be necessary nor sufficient. . . . As I would put it, while neither necessary nor sufficient for all clients, the core conditions are helpful to extremely helpful with virtually all clients. (2007, p. 592)

A recent issue of the journal *Psychotherapy: Theory, Research, Practice, Training* (2007) contained a special section in which 11 appraisals of Rogers's hypothesis were offered by a group of highly accomplished therapists from several schools of thought, including person-centered and humanistic. Each expert therapist was asked to comment on the impact, limitations, enduring aspects, and current influence of Rogers's seminal paper.

Of the 12 expert commentators (one article had coauthors), not one took the position that the conditions were necessary and sufficient for all clients, and the majority suggested that, while the conditions may be useful to many clients, they were not sufficient for most. One important criticism was that the relationship between the core therapist conditions of empathy, unconditional positive regard, and congruence together generally show a modest positive relationship to good client outcome. Based on the views of these expert commentators, as well as my own, I will offer a critical review of each of Rogers's six necessary and sufficient conditions.

Empathy

Therapist empathy is one of the most reliable predictors of good client outcome. However, as Bachelor (1988), Grote (2005), and others have noted, what clients experience as empathic varies from client to client and may take a number of forms. Thus, it appears that, for an empathic response to be maximally effective, it needs to match the client's view of empathy. This evidence is consistent with the research findings that client perceptions of a therapist behavior or attitude are better predictors of client outcome than therapist views of the same quality or behavior.

Brodley and Brody (1990) reported that 90% of Rogers's responses to clients were empathic. With such a strong focus on being empathic and responding to the client's reality, Rogers and most person-centered therapists respond predominantly in a one-sided style. In this classical form of empathic responding, the therapist often becomes so immersed in the client's experience that the person of the therapist remains in the background in what is essentially a "selfless" desire to understand. While this disciplined style serves to promote client reflection and understanding, it tends to preclude a focus on the therapist's reactions to the client. In contrast, by engaging in inclusion, person-centered therapists would empathically attune themselves to their clients' experience while also remaining aware of their own thoughts, feelings, and reactions and bring these forth for clients' consideration. Such authentic dialogue allows therapist and client to have a "meeting of their minds" that would generate varying perspectives of reality for clients to explore. Thus, therapist and client work as partners in cocreating the best understanding of the client's experience. At times, it is desirable for therapist and client to engage in metacommunication or conversation about what transpires between them and the therapeutic process. Since both therapist and client are part of the same field, and therefore inevitably influence each other, it would seem beneficial for each to examine and understand that impact. This would serve to demystify therapy and make possible more genuine dialogue about the how the therapist and client might work more effectively.

Unconditional Positive Regard

Therapist acceptance, unconditional positive regard, and affirmation are clearly constructive attitudes and behaviors from which clients benefit. However, a problem with the concept of unconditional positive regard in practice is that it simply cannot be consistently communicated if the therapist is authentic. Therapists, like all people, inevitably feel judgmental, critical, and disapproving at times. Difficult or unpleasant clients inevitably elicit negative reactions from therapists. None of us are so tolerant or saintly as to be completely unconditional in our regard for all clients no matter how they behave. Further, therapists cannot leave their values and sense of morality outside of therapy. Nor can they maintain some hypothetical state of neutrality. Consequently, therapists do not always feel unconditional positive regard for all clients any more than we can attain the same standards toward all of the persons we know. To attempt to do so renders the therapist incongruent, dishonest, and compromises his or her integrity with the client. Obviously, there is an inevitable tension between therapist positive regard and genuineness that requires judicious consideration before the therapist decides how to respond. Germain Lietaer has observed that:

> There is a potential conflict between genuineness or congruence on the one hand, and unconditionality on the other; it is a rare person and a rare time in which the constancy of acceptance can be provided for any therapist for any client. Thus, while unconditionality is not impossible, it is improbable. (Levant & Shlien, 1984, p. 41)

Although clients inevitably want to be accepted, they cannot possibly trust or find credible a therapist who condones or seems to accept all of their behaviors, however compromising, immoral, or heinous. To look the other way would do a disservice to our clients.

Mary Nicholas, author of *The Mystery of Goodness and the Positive Moral Consequences of Psychotherapy* (1994), takes the position that, "For the therapist to be neutral when the client is being immoral conveys to the client that the therapist does not have the courage of his convictions to risk the patient's outrage and defensiveness and confront an immorality" (p. 13). Moreover, there are times when moral issues are at the heart of the client's problems (e.g., cheating on one's spouse, child abuse, fire setting, physical and psychological mistreatment of others, illegal activities). There are instances when it is desirable for therapists to take a stand regarding what is in the best interests of persons other than the client (e.g., Tarasoff-type situations where potential victims must be warned).

Values and character development are important parts of therapy that are of concern to the client. Therefore, there are times when therapists best serve their clients by engaging them in considering such value questions as: "Is your behavior compatible with the person you want to be?"

or "How will you feel about yourself if you engage in x behavior?" Client guilt and shame are often vital to process because such reactions suggest that the client has violated his or her own values and standards. Sometimes our genuine concern for the client's well-being may take precedence over absolute unconditionality. During a session with a long-term client who was expressing embarrassment about his girlfriend's ballet dancing skills (he is an accomplished and professional ballet dancer), I noticed myself feeling a little annoyed with him. I decided to share this annoyance and then checked to assess how it was received. My client expressed his appreciation for my comment, which reflected his own dissatisfaction with himself for being critical of his less-skilled girlfriend. While this interchange was a bit risky, therapists and clients often do not share with each other their negative feelings; consequently, the integrity of the relationship is compromised, and relationship strains and ruptures sometimes occur. When such difficult and "touchy" sentiments can be shared, processed, and worked though, the quality of the relationship is often made stronger. Conversely, when such conflicts are kept underground, either to avoid conflict or to spare the other's feelings, the relationship becomes more distant, cautious, and superficial.

Just because the therapist's regard cannot realistically be unconditional in all instances does not mean that the therapist can't be consistently "for" his or her client. As long as the therapist's commitment to the client remains unwavering, it is possible for therapists to value, support, feel compassion for, and care about their clients regardless of aspects of clients' personality and behavior that the therapist doesn't like or condone. Mearns and Thorne (2007) articulate their position that "valuing the client as a person of worth is not conditional—it is equally possible to feel that deep valuing of the humanity of a person who displays a pattern of values quite different from our own" (p. 97).

Congruence

Rogers considered congruence to be the most essential condition of the three core therapist responses or ways of being. Therapist congruence or genuineness often elicits trust, facilitates genuine meeting, and serves as a model for client congruence. However, research suggests that, while congruence shows a modest relationship to client change, it sometimes shows no relationship or a *negative* one (Sachse & Elliott, 2002). In short, therapist congruence is the weakest of the three core therapist conditions in terms of its relationship to good outcome and is fraught with potential problems for therapist and client.

Experts in the field of psychotherapy have wrestled with Rogers's emphasis on the central role of congruence in therapy. Hill (2007) suggests that "more attention be paid to therapist self-awareness and how therapists decide what to do about negative feelings" (pp. 261–262). Wachtel (2007) takes the position that "congruence or genuineness is perhaps the most complex and difficult of the six conditions to understand conceptually and master in daily practice. It points to vexing questions with which therapists continue to struggle" (p. 280). He points out that troubling therapist feelings such as anger, sexual attraction, and other problematic reactions may undermine the unconditionality of the therapist's positive regard. Samstag (2007) questions how real the therapist's genuineness can be "considering that that it is devoid of true interpersonal reciprocity and denies the power of the therapist" (p. 298). As is increasingly evident, being transparent poses many challenges for which there are no simple answers. As was discussed earlier, therapist transparency and disclosure may be for better or worse and will usually come with an unpredictable amount of risk.

Client Perception of Core Therapist Conditions

Rogers showed great prescience in understanding that, unless therapist empathy, unconditional positive regard, and congruence are perceived by the client, they do not have the expected impact. Although all person-centered therapists understand that the core conditions must be perceived to be effective, a review of transcripts indicates that therapists rarely inquire about or confirm the existence of such conditions in their clients. Nor do clients indicate very often that such conditions are evident to them. Since most person-centered therapists rarely, if ever, confirm that their clients perceive that the conditions are provided to them, they may not exist at all in clients' perceptions or, if they do, the quality or impact of the conditions offered is unknown to therapists. Further, therapists are often poor judges of their own therapeutic behavior and overestimate the constructive impact they have on clients. This makes it even more essential that therapists meta-communicate with clients about their experience of therapy.

This problem is further complicated by the fact that what clients think of as empathy, unconditional positive regard, and congruence may not correspond to the form in which therapists believe they have communicated these conditions (e.g., Bachelor, 1988). Miller, Duncan, and Hubble (1997) make a convincing argument that the manner in which the therapist's relational qualities are communicated needs to fit the client's view and experience of those qualities. Thus, the core conditions need to be varied to fit each client's view of the conditions. This can only happen if therapists metacommunicate with their clients or use some other form of feedback (e.g., relationship inventory) to assess clients' experiences in therapy.

Psychological Contact

Point 1 of Rogers's hypothesis is that two persons are in psychological contact and that a minimal relationship exists. Rogers did not elaborate this condition though others have done so. In many humanistic therapies, the quality of contact or engagement between therapist and client is a core aspect of the therapeutic process. On the therapist's side, the quality of therapist *presence* and focused immersion in the client often have a powerful impact. Contact is a core aspect of pretherapy (Prouty, VanWerde, & Portner, 2002) for severely impaired clients. Suffice it to say that this condition was not well defined by Rogers or adequately operationalized for research purposes. Qualities similar or related to contact identified by therapy researchers include the therapist's contribution to the therapist–client bond and therapist quality of engagement (as opposed to detachment). In short, clients will benefit from therapists' monitoring and insuring that the quality of contact and engagement with their clients is sufficient.

Client Incongruence or Anxiety

Point 2 of Rogers's hypothesis is that the client is in a state of incongruence, being vulnerable or anxious. As Neil Watson (1984) has pointed out, Rogers's necessary and sufficient conditions hypothesis, as stated, has never been fully tested by outcome research because the conditions of psychological contact and client incongruence have not been included. A state of incongruence or anxiety is likely to motivate some clients to engage in therapy and seek relief from their distresses. However, clinical observation and experience suggest that it is unlikely that a state of anxiety or incongruence is sufficient to bring clients to therapy or adequately motivate them to remain invested in therapy or to grapple with arduous problems in their lives. Some clients even prefer to drop out of therapy and live with their anxieties and troubles rather than undergo the difficulties inherent in therapeutic change.

One Size Can't Fit All

A questionable premise of Rogers's hypothesis is that the core therapist qualities are sufficient for all varieties of clients and problems, implying that one size fits all and that there is no need for the therapist to do more than be empathic, congruent, and accepting, a belief still held by many person-centered therapists. Simple logic and clinical experience suggest that neither person-centered nor any other type of therapy, without some modifications, is sufficient to assist clients with a vast array of psychopathological conditions and experiences, especially those whose problems are severe and/or chronic and those with a strong biological component (e.g., bipolar or obsessive-compulsive disorder).

Lazarus (2007) contends that the core conditions are inadequate to help clients with a variety of deficits such as dysfunctional beliefs, inadequate or missing information, misinformation, and deficits in social skills. He points out the need for individualization and states: "A flexible and versatile clinician is fully cognizant that *necessity and sufficiency are individualistic and depend largely on the personal needs of and expectancies of each individual client*" (p. 253, italics added). Along the same lines Silberschatz (2007) comments that "by prescribing the same set of conditions for all patients, it is paradoxically lacking in case specificity" (p. 266). Samstag (2007) suggests that Rogers' core therapist qualities "do not necessarily serve a uniformly facilitative function across all clients; for certain clients, a therapist's empathy will be supportive and facilitative, whereas for others it may not be experienced that way" (p. 298).

One could fairly argue that the core conditions, without modification, are of limited effectiveness for problems such as autism, chronic schizophrenia, obsessive-compulsive disorder, bipolar disorder, panic disorder, ADHD, sleep disorders, and a variety of health problems (e.g., chronic pain) for which specific techniques have proven to be effective (e.g., exposure for phobias). Further, Rogers's theory does not acknowledge the critical influence that genetics or temperament may have on clients and client functioning or how such factors might require alterations in the therapist's approach.

Another problem not adequately addressed by Rogers and many person-centered practitioners is that of clients who lack motivation for change, adequate involvement and participation, or sufficient effort to change. There are a variety of clients who are characterized, in varying degrees, by passivity, avoidance, dependence, denial of problems evident to others, or an expectation or hope that others will take care of them. Some clients take little responsibility for improving their lives. They seem to be stuck in their own inertia and have little inclination to maintain or improve their functioning. They prefer to avoid the discomfort and stress of making an effort to improve their functioning or the discouragement of failing if they do try. Consequently, clients who seem to be more motivated to minimize stress and discomfort by narrowing their worlds and avoiding anything that seems difficult remain a challenge for therapists of all persuasions.

Equivalence of the Effectiveness of Psychotherapy

The well-established fact that major schools of thought are roughly equivalent in their effectiveness suggests that other relational factors and therapeutic procedures are at play. Some therapies such as behavior therapy rely relatively little on Rogers's core relational variables. Alvin Mahrer (2007) contends that, "Rogers' necessary and sufficient conditions are irrelevant for my experiential psychotherapy and perhaps for many other therapies as well" (p. 275). If extremely diverse therapeutic approaches vary considerably in the way therapy is practiced, then the argument can be made that Rogers's core conditions are neither necessary nor sufficient for all clients. The simple fact that most people deal with their problems without the help of a therapist and that many troubled persons benefit from self-help materials and self-help groups further call into question the necessity of the core conditions.

LOOKING FORWARD: REKINDLING ROGERS'S PIONEERING SPIRIT

While most person-centered scholars and practitioners, myself included, continue to acknowledge Rogers's seminal and profound contributions to the field of psychotherapy, his belief that there was still much to be learned has not been adequately appreciated and embraced. Consequently, there is a need for members of our international person-centered community to continue to take a fresh and critical look at Rogers's theory and the extensive body of psychotherapy research and practice that could enhance it. Toward this end, I hope to rekindle Rogers's pioneering spirit and offer some proposals for the future

When Rogers published in 1959 "A Theory of Therapy, Personality, and Interpersonal Relationships, as Developed in the Client-Centered Framework," he issued the following cautions that have largely been ignored to this day by most students of client/person-centered theory. Rogers warned:

> I believe that there is only one statement which can accurately apply to all theories . . . from the theory I will present to the one which *I hope will replace it in a decade*—and that is that *at the time of its formulation every theory contains an unknown* (and perhaps at that point an unknowable) *amount of error and mistaken inference*. The degree of error may be very great . . . or small, . . . *but unless we regard the discovery of truth as a closed and finished book, then there will be new discoveries which will contradict the best theories which we can now construct.*
>
> To me this attitude is very important, for I am distressed at the manner in which small-caliber minds immediately accept a theory—almost any theory—as a dogma of truth. If theory could be seen for what it is— a fallible, changing attempt to construct a network of gossamer threads which will contain the solid facts—then a theory would serve as it

should, as a stimulus to further creative thinking . . . *at the time a theory is constructed, some precautions should be taken to prevent it from becoming dogma.* (italics added, pp. 190–191)

TOWARD A COLLABORATIVE PERSON-CENTERED PSYCHOTHERAPY: REFORMULATING ROGERS'S NECESSARY AND SUFFICIENT CONDITIONS HYPOTHESIS

In the spirit of Rogers's open-minded receptivity to new information and evidence, I offer a reformulation and expansion of his hypothesis. These ideas evolved over 20 years of reflection about Rogers's position. The following proposal is firmly rooted in and built on Rogers's theory of psychotherapy, especially the conditions he proposed to effect constructive change in the client. The model proposed draws heavily from research in person-centered and humanistic–existential therapies and from many of the advances articulated by some of the leading scholars and practitioners of person-centered therapy. It also draws from a body of knowledge in the larger field of psychotherapy. It is informed by various descriptions of the therapeutic alliance (Kirschenbaum, 2007) that articulate the importance of (a) therapist collaboration, (b) the client's belief that therapy will be effective, (c) a mutual understanding of how therapist and client will work together, (d) the client's affective relationship with the therapist, (e) the client's capacity to work purposefully in therapy, (f) therapist empathic understanding and involvement, and (g) agreement on the goals and tasks of therapy.

This formulation is intended to broaden the scope of what it means to be person-centered and expand the range of effective practice. The proposal represents my attempt to integrate ideas from the variations in person-centered therapies described earlier in this text. A core and pervasive premise in the position I am proposing is that of *therapist–client collaboration*. A major shift evident in the field of psychotherapy is that therapists are moving toward increasingly involving their clients in all aspects of the therapy, an approach advocated in the American Psychological Association's Presidential Task Force on Evidence-Based Practice: "psychotherapy is a collaborative enterprise in which patients and clinicians negotiate ways of working together that are mutually agreeable and likely to lead to positive outcomes" (Vollmer, Grote, Lange, & Walker, 2009, p. 34). The preliminary findings of the task force indicate that clients liked being offered choices and found it important to be included in the decision-making process about their therapy.

Another guiding principle in the reformulation is to *do whatever is in the best interests of the client*, regardless of whether it fits with the person-centered theory from which one operates currently. This proposal is founded on a primary commitment to the client's well-being and guided by a pragmatism that draws on whatever provides the best evidence or holds the most promise for assisting our clients.

Finally, I offer this reformulation in a tentative manner that is subject to further modification in the light of new research, theory, and innovations in practice.

Optimal Conditions for Constructive Therapeutic Change

1. *The client is sufficiently distressed in an area of significant relevance, has a desire for help, and willingly seeks professional assistance in the alleviation of problems or to attain something the client wants.*

Most people do not seek psychotherapy unless their level of psychological distress is intolerable or at least unacceptable. While anxiety or incongruence may be an adequate reason for some persons to enter or continue therapy and to motivate change, most persons tolerate varying levels of psychological discomfort on their own and consequently do not seek therapeutic assistance. Further, when the level of discomfort diminishes to a tolerable level, many clients drop out of therapy. The dropout rate for clients varies from about 40% to as high as 67% (e.g., Clarkin & Levy, 2004) and the modal number of sessions attended by clients is one. Clearly many persons who might enter or continue in therapy will not do so unless they are sufficiently troubled and desirous of change.

The experience of being "sufficiently distressed" reflects clients' subjective sense that their problems, however defined, are no longer bearable and interfere their functioning or quality of life to an unacceptable degree. The level of psychic discomfort will vary but will be characterized by a sense of urgency to alleviate stress or attain something in an area deemed important enough (e.g., finding purpose in life) to seek professional assistance. Further, the person feels unable to deal with distress on his or her own and recognizes a need for assistance, has a desire to be helped, and willingly seeks and accepts help. Subjectively, the potential client is likely to experience something like, "I am extremely unhappy and cannot deal with this important issue on my own. I need and want help." Persons experiencing such psychological states are likely to seek psychotherapy willingly and be receptive to ongoing assistance. In short, therapy is likely to be more successful when clients freely choose to attend based on an unacceptable level of distress.

2. *The client is actively involved and receptive in the therapeutic endeavor, participates cooperatively, and has a positive expectation that therapy will be helpful.*

As mentioned earlier, Rogers basically left client responsibility for therapy participation and change out of his formula. In the last few decades, accumulating evidence regarding the critical role of the client in change has dramatically altered our understanding of the importance of client involvement in successful outcome. As veteran researchers Bergin and Garfield (1984) concluded after reviewing decades of psychotherapy research,

> it is the client more than the therapist who implements the change process. If the client does not absorb, utilize and follow through on the facilitative efforts of the therapist, then nothing happens. Rather than argue over whether or not "therapy works," we could address ourselves to the question of whether or not "the client works"! . . . Clients are not inert objects upon whom techniques are administered. . . . People are agentic beings who are effective forces in the complex of causal events . . . . As therapists have depended more upon the client's resources, more change seems to occur. (p. 826)

Despite the fact that most reasonably well-trained and competent therapists of varying persuasions offer clients something of value to promote learning and growth, some clients fail to make use of whatever the therapist provides. It appears that clients' involvement and active participation in therapy play a large role in whether or not they progress. Research shows that client role engagement or personal involvement is a strong predictor of good outcome. In a series of 54 outcome studies, 65% showed a positive relationship to good outcome (Sachse & Elliott, 2002). From the therapist's perspective, 92% of findings show a significant positive relationship to outcome (Orlinsky et al., 1994). Art Bohart, a respected person-centered therapist and coauthor of *How Clients Make Therapy Work* (1999), cites considerable evidence that client involvement in therapy is the most important factor making therapy effective and that therapists should support, stimulate, and encourage client investment in therapy.

As defined here, client involvement entails client cooperative engagement and commitment to the therapy process. It also suggests that clients take responsibility for themselves, attend sessions as scheduled, have a focus and goals, come prepared to engage their issues, and are receptive to learning and change. Research indicates that client openness (i.e., willingness to disclose and process problematic aspects of experience and self), versus defensiveness, is related to good outcome in 80% of studies (Orlinsky et al., 1994). Similarly, research shows a significant association with positive outcome for cooperative participation, client motivation, or desire for therapeutic involvement and clients' behavioral and cognitive processing (Orlinsky et al., 1994). The evidence seems clear: When clients are active and involved participants, they are likely to make progress.

3. *The therapist and client are mutually accepting and affirming.*

This premise expands on Rogers's belief about the constructive effects of therapist unconditional positive regard by suggesting that mutual acceptance and affirmation are more powerful than just the therapist's acceptance of the client. Clients don't work well with therapists they don't like. Nor do therapists work well with clients they don't like since the quality of their relationship is likely to be compromised or strained. Client affirmation, defined as respect and liking for the therapist, is positively related to outcome in about 69% of the studies while therapist affirmation of the client (acceptance, warmth, or positive regard) is associated with positive outcome in 56% of 154 studies (Orlinsky et al., 1994). Reciprocal affirmation between therapist and client is significantly and positively related to outcome in 78% of 32 studies (Orlinsky et al., 1994). It would appear that when client and therapist are mutually affirming, clients are most likely to achieve constructive change.

4. *The therapist is consistently present and actively engaged in all aspects of the therapeutic process.*

On several occasions, I had the opportunity to view Carl Rogers close up when he did therapeutic demonstrations. I was struck by his exceptional capacity to concentrate on the client before him. It was as if he and the client entered an impenetrable bubble in which only they existed, despite the fact that they were being watched by a large number of observers. The quality of Rogers's contact and engagement with his client was extraordinary. He simply brought all of himself fully to his client, without wavering, and trusted that the sheer quality of his "being with" his client had healing potential. Rogers commented about his presence:

> I find that when I am the closest to my inner, intuitive self—when perhaps I am in touch with the unknown in me—when perhaps I am in a slightly altered state of consciousness in the relationship, then whatever I do seems to be full of healing Then simply my presence is releasing and helpful. (Baldwin, 1987, p. 50)

When present in this manner described by Rogers, clients are often drawn into moments of fully engaged and present living with their therapists, an experience that is gratifying, meaningful, hopeful, instructive, and sometimes transformative as they glimpse the possibility of carrying such experiences into their relationships with others. Clients also learn that the quality of their lives in general is enhanced by living fully in the present.

When fully present, therapists bring a sustained, mindful, and focused attention to their clients. They make powerful contact and immerse themselves in their clients' worlds and draw their clients into a meaningful encounter. They are fully and transparently themselves in the moment and without any agenda except to be with and receive their clients, thereby creating a sense of safety that enables them to disclose themselves more fully. When present, the therapist *indwells* the client's world, is *for* the client and is *with* the client as a separate self who is willing to engage in an I–Thou encounter (Moustakas, 1995). A variety of therapist relational qualities and behaviors related to presence have been supported by 40 years of research (e.g., Asay & Lambert, 1999). Research shows that client perception of the therapist's contribution to the therapeutic bond or alliance was related to positive outcome in 67% of studies and was never negatively associated with outcome when viewed from the client's perspective (Sachse & Elliott, 2002). Similarly, the client's contribution to the bond was positively significant and positively associated with outcome in 67% of 55 studies suggesting, again, that clients affect their therapists' quality of presence (Orlinsky et al., 1994d). Presence-related research by Elliott (1985) suggested that effective therapists focused on client problems, paid attention to affect, helped clients focus their awareness and become more involved, and maintained personal contact.

5. *The therapist views clients as resourceful persons capable of constructive change and strives to support their freedom and autonomy in determining the direction of therapy and how their goals will be achieved.*

Rogers believed that the actualizing tendency in clients would be optimized when they experienced an interpersonal environment characterized by adequate levels of empathy, acceptance, and congruence in their therapists. Similarly, Bohart and Tallman (1999) make a compelling argument that therapy is a learning process and that engaging the client's self-healing potential is essential in helping them. Further, evidence presented by Bohart and Tallman (1999) suggests that most people/clients manage their lives adequately without the assistance of professional helpers by drawing on their own and other resources (e.g., self-help books, supportive friends and family, and other readily available resources).

Lambert's research (1992) indicated that about 40% of outcome in therapy was related to client resources, while another 15% of outcome is accounted for by clients' positive expectation and hope that therapy will be helpful. Such hopefulness is strongly influenced by the therapist's optimism and conviction that clients can mobilize their resources for change.

As therapists embrace this view, they depend more on their clients to deal with their problems. This clearly shifts therapists' responsibility from effecting change to that of facilitating clients' capacity to mobilize their current resources and potential for change.

Person-centered therapists place a high value on encouraging and supporting client freedom and autonomy in decision making about what they wish to change and how such change might be achieved. This value emerges naturally from the person-centered therapist's belief that clients have the right to choose what they want and how to conduct their lives without undo influence, guidance, advice, or specific suggestions for change.

6. *The therapist and client individualize each therapy by being collaborative partners in the definition of the client's problems, desired goals, means to achieve those goals, and development of an optimal therapeutic relationship.*

A compelling argument can be made that no one knows the client better than the client. Thus, clients are the best experts on themselves, and this belief is critical for the therapist to work effectively with the client. Therefore, I contend that therapists cannot maintain that clients knows what is best for them and, at the same time, define, a priori, what specific conditions are necessary and sufficient for all clients. Similarly, I would consider a prescription for therapist nondirectiveness under all circumstances to present the same dilemma. Each client and each course of therapy are unique. Further, clients need and benefit from different things at different times. Therefore, each course of therapy needs to be cocreated by therapist and client as it evolves to increase the likelihood of client benefit. Although clients take the lead in deciding what problems are to be addressed and their related goals, therapists and clients work together in defining and creating an optimal therapeutic relationship and course of therapy to achieve those goals.

Research reported earlier indicates that client perceptions of therapist behavior are better predictors of outcome than those of the therapist or external judges. Bachelor's research (1985) showed that what the client defines as empathy varies from client to client and that the therapist needs to ensure that qualities and behaviors beneficial to the client are perceived/experienced. Grote's (2005) qualitative research on "feeling understood" shows that multiple therapist qualities and behaviors other than empathic ones contributed to this experience. Rennie's (2002) qualitative research shows that clients are self-aware agents in therapy and therefore respond in their own ways to the therapist's responses and proposals. Further, it appears that clients creatively use whatever their therapists offer them selectively and in their own way (Rennie, 2002). These studies and others like them make a compelling case that therapists need to remain constantly mindful of what is likely to best serve the client at a given time. If therapists take the role of learners in relationship to their clients, they are likely to observe and inquire about what is needed or likely to be most fruitful in specific situations. Clinical wisdom and many prominent therapists (e.g., Lazarus) point to the importance of individualizing therapy. It is the therapist's responsibility to adapt and accommodate in a manner that works best for a given client. Therapists' metacommunication about therapy is vital in helping them know what fits and works for a specific client. I have found that incorporating a post-session dialogue with the client is often helpful in providing mutual feedback about how therapy is progressing and what adaptations or changes might be desirable or necessary on the part of the therapist or client.

7. *The therapist understands the subjective reality of the client and empathically communicates that understanding to the client.*

Constant therapist empathic attunement remains the bedrock of all versions of person-centered psychotherapies. Therapists of every school of thought understand that empathy, in various forms, is foundational for developing a therapeutic alliance with their clients, in catalyzing client interpersonal and intrapersonal learning, and in achieving good outcomes. Empathy, as perceived by the client, was associated with positive outcome in 72% of 47 studies (Orlinsky et al., 1994). The majority of studies show a positive correlation between therapist empathy and outcome, and no studies shows a negative relationship between therapist empathy and outcome. Feeling understood is one of the primary experiences clients identify as being helpful. Rogers's greatest contribution to the field of psychotherapy is that he taught us to listen, enter the client's world, and communicate that understanding for the client's reflection. This contribution remains as vital as ever.

8. *The therapist engages relevant aspects of his or her self in a congruent manner intended to be in the best interests of the client.*

The therapist–client relationship itself often creates growth-enhancing experiences in the client. Thus, it is essential that therapists engage various aspects of themselves on behalf of their clients. The greater the depth and range of the therapist, the more the therapist has to offer the client. Although person-centered theory suggests that therapist empathy, congruence, and acceptance are sufficient qualities for client growth, both research evidence and clinical experience indicate that other qualities enhance the relationship and provide personal resources that benefit the client.

One of the professors in my master's program said something that has always remained with me: "You can best be yourself and nobody else." The best way therapists can engage themselves on behalf of the client is to be themselves. The person you are during therapy should largely resemble the person your best friends and family know. When therapists express various aspects of themselves in a genuine manner, clients come to know and trust the person of the therapist. This often results in a more involved relationship that allows clients to share and be more themselves.

Engaging in a therapeutic relationship with our clients provides us with an opportunity to be the best of our selves. Each of us has distinctive personal qualities that are likely to enhance our relationships with our clients and effect change. The challenge for therapists is to know who they are and bring forward those aspects of self that serve the best interests of their clients.

9. *The therapist brings forth for the client's consideration any and all personal and professional resources that may be of value to the client.*

Clients want and deserve to have available to them all aspects of the therapist's personal qualities, skills, professional knowledge, and resources, just as we should expect no less from our physicians. When clients come to therapy, they typically indicate that they hope we will understand them, be supportive and caring, help them understand themselves, and deal more effectively with their concerns. They often express a desire to attain some tools or skills to help them cope and function better. In some cases our clients don't know what they need to help them think, feel, and do better, but they certainly recognize what is helpful and what is not. Thus, person-centered therapists would do well to depend on their clients to assess the value of whatever their therapists might offer. If we collaborate with our clients effectively, we will learn together what will benefit our clients and how to achieve it.

Person-centered therapists operate from a theoretical framework that provides cohesiveness to their belief system and guidelines for practice. In my view, this is fully appropriate as it enables them to work from a set of convictions that grounds their therapy with their clients. Yet all theories, person-centered included, have limitations and need to be modified to adapt to the needs of clients.

While I fully believe that therapists should be grounded in their therapeutic beliefs and values, theoretical allegiance should never limit therapists from doing what is in the best interests of their clients, regardless of whether it fits or diverges from their theory of psychotherapy. As mentioned previously in this text, there are problems for which person-centered therapy is not ideally suited, at least not without supplementation or modification. I contend that therapeutic pragmatism, or doing "what works" is an ethical and professional responsibility. Most clients care little about our theoretical predilections and rarely inquire about them, since their primary concern is whether we can assist them with their problems.

Doing what works or what is in the best interests of a given client may take various forms. Since therapists' fundamental commitment is to their clients' well-being, it is appropriate and desirable that they bring forth their perspectives, values, beliefs, perceptions, knowledge, relational skills, and therapeutic processes and procedures for their client's consideration. As a collaborative partner the therapist offers, but does not insist on, whatever he or she believes may be of most value to the client. Such a therapeutic approach would be more client-directed and client-informed and thus truly more client-centered in the sense that the client is always an active and agentic participant in the therapy. This model of person-centered therapy would alter the premise that therapists remain absolutely nondirective in their approach to clients since doing so may restrict the availability of the therapist's professional and personal resources. In this approach therapists are free to offer noncoercively whatever is believed to be in their clients' best interests while clients are ultimately free to choose what fits and reject what doesn't. As suggested in dialogical approaches, there are times when it is appropriate for therapist and client to "wrestle" with each other in an effort to help the client achieve clarity in choosing the optimal course to take in his or her life.

As existential therapist Clark Moustakas (1995) concluded, there are times when it may be more important for the client to make the best decision possible rather than a freely made decision that may have unwanted consequences. In this approach, an optimal course for the client is likely to be based on consideration of all the available perspectives, options, and resources.

10. *The therapist focuses on and encourages the client to attend to and process potent emotional experiences with an intent to facilitate adaptive client learning and more effective behavior.*

A compelling argument can be made that meaningful experience is embodied, that we experience our world through our body, that the body "knows" more than can be articulated initially, and that we cannot fully grasp our realities without access to the meaning of our bodily felt senses. Most problems that trouble clients have a strong emotional component. Person-centered/experiential approaches to therapy view emotion as a critical source of adaptive learning, good judgment, and effective decision making. When affective and cognitive appraisal converge (i.e., when a possible course of behavior sounds right and feels right), the client is more likely to choose an effective course of action. Therefore, giving high priority to helping clients attend to and process emotion is in clients' best interests.

There is a substantial and growing body of research that demonstrates that effective processing of client emotion and bodily felt experiences leads to good outcome. Recent process research (Elliott, Watson, Goldman, & Greenberg, 2004) has consistently demonstrated a relationship between in-session emotional activation and outcome in various therapies. Emotion-focused therapy in particular has a sound base of research demonstrating the importance of processing emotion to good outcome.

Research on depth of experiencing in therapy has been shown consistently to relate to outcome, especially in client-centered therapy (Greenberg et al., 2002). Warwar and Greenberg's (1999) research indicated that clients with good outcomes in the treatment of depression showed both higher emotional arousal and depth of experiencing on emotion episodes. Alvin Mahrer and colleagues (Mahrer, Nadler, Dessaulles, Gervaize, & Sterner, 1987) have shown that certain good moments in therapy are characterized by emotional expression. Other studies have found similar results showing a relation between emotional experiencing and outcome in therapy (Beutler, 1999; Foa & Jacob, 1998; Greenberg & Foster, 1996; Hirscheimer, 1995; Malcolm, 1999; Orlinsky et al., 1994; Paivio & Greenberg, 1995). In brief, the evidence is strong and growing that working effectively with client emotion leads to good outcome. One should note, however, that emotional arousal alone is not sufficient, and good outcomes are distinguished from poor ones by clients making sense of their emotions. In short, emotional experiences need to be aroused, processed, and reflected upon cognitively for optimal benefit.

11. *The therapist continuously monitors the quality of the therapeutic relationship, client progress, and any strains in the relationship and collaborates with the client to make any needed or desirable adjustments.*

Research from several sources indicates that clients' and therapists' views of the same therapy are often discrepant, sometimes substantially so. In fact, studies often show that therapists are not good judges of their own behavior and impact on the client, often overestimating their effectiveness. As Rennie's research (2002) showed, clients often do not share their views of the therapist or therapy. Therefore, the responsibility for monitoring the therapy falls to the therapist. This should be an ongoing part of therapy that is done at frequent intervals. In the last few years, my graduate students and I have found that a post-session dialogue with the client at the end of each session can be extremely useful in assessing how the therapy is going and to stimulate productive discussion about what adjustments may be desirable. Therapists would do well to converse with their clients at any time they sense that something is awry. Such input is especially valuable when there are strains and potential ruptures in the therapist–client relationship. Safran, Muran, and Samstag, (1994) have noted that successful therapy is often characterized by a rupture–repair cycle in the therapeutic alliance that may occur at any time during therapy. However, it tends to occur when the therapist begins to address maladaptive client patterns. Such ruptures may also occur as a result of therapist criticism, indifference, and dislike of the client. Their findings suggest that therapist focus on the client's feelings about the therapy and the therapist is crucial in repairing the rupture and that failure to address such ruptures will likely lead to increased client negativity and unsuccessful outcomes. While it may take some time, effort, and courage for therapists to assess how therapy is going from the client's perspective, such information is vital in keeping the therapy on track and thriving.

12. *The client experiences in the therapist the relevant constructive relational qualities, behaviors, and intents to a degree that facilitates change and growth as defined by the client.*

Rogers was aware that for therapy to be effective, the core conditions needed to be perceived or experienced by the client to be effective. Both research and clinical experience suggest that several therapist qualities, attitudes, and behaviors lead to constructive therapeutic change in the client. However, since each client and course of therapy is unique, it is essential that the therapist is aware that what is important for each client to benefit optimally from therapy will vary. What matters most to a given client (e.g., feeling supported or encouraged) will vary, and when the specific constellation of therapeutic qualities and behaviors needed by the client to use therapy effectively are offered and perceived, then therapeutic effectiveness will be increased.

SUMMARY

In an era characterized by increasing technology, multitasking, overly busy and stressed lives, depersonalization, and medication as a first choice for alleviation of a variety of debilitating psychological problems, person-centered therapies become increasingly needed and relevant. A therapy that stresses the importance of the quality of relationship and that encourages clients to listen to themselves and to live in a more self-accepting and authentic manner will always be needed. Good ideas, like good art, endure. Rogers's system of psychotherapy has endured for 70 years, and the therapist qualities of empathy, congruence, and unconditional positive regard have been acknowledged by almost every major system of psychotherapy as fundamental contributors to clients' growth.

Today person-centered therapy continues to be an influential force in the larger field of psychotherapy. As you will recall, Rogers was identified as the most influential therapist of any era in surveys conducted in 1982 and 2007. Today, Rogers's influence on American psychotherapy is enormous, though often indirect. His fundamental ideas have been absorbed by many diverse approaches to psychotherapy. A substantial number of training programs for graduate students in psychology and counseling typically emphasize the importance of empathic listening and responding skills and attitudes, as well as the critical importance of unconditional positive regard for the client and therapist congruence. Rogers, more than any other therapist, taught us to listen with sensitivity and caring and to understand that the quality of the therapist–client relationship, in itself, has the potential to foster personal learning and growth in the client.

Globally, person-centered therapy flourishes in the United Kingdom, many European countries, South America, Japan, and increasingly in Russia and China. In their article "The Current Status of Carl Rogers and the Person-Centered Approach" (2005), Kirchenbaum and Jourdan indicate that between 1987 and 2004, a total of 777 person-centered publications, including 141 books, were published. This total far exceeds all of the previous publications over the 40-year period from 1946 to 1986. Further, there are approximately 200 person-centered organizations and training centers worldwide. Kirschenbaum and Jourdan conclude: "By all these indicators, the person-centered approach is . . . alive and well" and "client-centered principles permeate the practice of many, if not most therapists" (p. 48). Person-centered therapy is as vital and effective as it has ever been and continues to develop in ways that will make it increasingly so in the years to come.

Glossary of Key Terms

ACTUALIZING TENDENCY   The inherent tendency of the organism to develop all its capacities in ways that serve to maintain or enhance the organism.

CONDITIONS OF WORTH   Circumstances of self-experience that a person either seeks out or avoids because of his or her discrimination that the experience is more or less worthy of self-regard.

CONGRUENCE   A state in which the person's self-concept and experiences, including thoughts and behavior, are in harmony.

EMPATHY   The process of accurately perceiving the internal frame of reference of another, including both the emotional aspects and meaning of the experience.

EXTERNAL FRAME OF REFERENCE   Perception of the person solely from one's own subjective internal frame of reference without empathizing with the observed person.

INCONGRUENCE   State of discord between self-concept and experience.

INTERNAL FRAME OF REFERENCE   All of the realm of experience available to the awareness of the individual at a given moment; the subjective experience of the person.

LOCUS OF EVALUATION   Refers to the source of the person's values. If the source is internal, the person is the center of the valuing process, with the evidence supplied by his or her own senses. When the locus of evaluation resides in others, their judgment as to the value of an experience becomes the criterion of value for the individual.

ORGANISMIC VALUING PROCESS   Built-in, trustworthy, evaluative mechanism that enables the organism to experience satisfaction in those behaviors that maintain and enhance the organism and the self.

POSITIVE REGARD   Exists when a person perceives that some aspect of his or her behavior makes a positive difference to someone else.

PSYCHOLOGICAL ADJUSTMENT   Exists when self-concept is such that all experiences are or may be assimilated on a symbolic level into the gestalt of the self-structure.

PSYCHOLOGICAL MALADJUSTMENT   Exists when the organism denies awareness or experiences distortion in awareness of significant experiences, which consequently are not accurately symbolized and organized into the gestalt of the self-structure, thus creating incongruence between self and experience.

SELF, SELF-CONCEPT   The organized, consistent conceptual gestalt composed of perceptions of characteristics of the "I" or "me" together with the values attached to those perceptions.

SELF-ACTUALIZATION   Actualization of aspects of experience defined as the self.

UNCONDITIONAL POSITIVE REGARD   Exists when we perceive that any self-experience is viewed as worthy by another person.

Suggested Readings

Bohart, A. C., & Greenberg, L. S. (1997). *Empathy reconsidered: New directions in psychotherapy.* Washington, DC: American Psychological Association.

Bozarth, J., Zimring, F., & Tausch, R. (2002). Research in client-centered therapy: The evolution of a revolution. In D. J. Cain & J. Seeman (Eds.), *Humanistic psychotherapies: Handbook of research and practice.* Washington, DC: American Psychological Association.

Cain, D. J. (2002). *Classics in the person-centered approach.* Herefordshire, England: PCCS Books.

Cooper, M. (2007). Developmental and personality theory. In M. Cooper, M. O'Hara, P. F. Schmid, & G. Wyatt (Eds.), *The handbook of person-centered psychotherapy and counseling* (pp. 77–92). New York, NY: Palgrave Macmillan.

Cooper, M., O'Hara, M., Schmid, P. F., & Wyatt, G. (Eds.). (2007). *The handbook of person-centered psychotherapy and counseling.* New York, NY: Palgrave Macmillan.

Elliott, R., Watson, J. C., Goldman, R. N., & Greenberg, L. S. (2004). *Learning emotion focused therapy.* Washington, DC: American Psychological Association.

Gelso, C. J. (Ed.). (2007). The necessary and sufficient conditions at the half century mark. *Psychotherapy, 44*(3), 239–299.

Gendlin, E. T. (1996). *Focusing-oriented psychotherapy.* New York, NY: Guilford Press.

Greenberg, L. S., Watson, J. C., & Lietaer, G. (1998). *Handbook of experiential psychotherapy.* New York, NY: Guilford Press.

Kirschenbaum, H. (2007). *The life and work of Carl Rogers.* Ross-on-Wye, England: PCCS Books.

Mearns, D., & Thorne, B. (2007). *Person-centered counseling in action* (3rd ed.). London, England: Sage.

Rogers, C. R. (1951). *Client-centered psychotherapy.* Boston, MA: Houghton Mifflin.

Rogers, C. R. (1961). *On becoming a person.* Boston, MA: Houghton Mifflin.

Rogers, C. R. (1980). *A way of being*. Boston, MA: Houghton Mifflin.

Watson, J. C., Goldman, R. N., & Warner, M. S. (2002). *Client-centered and experiential psychotherapy in the 21st century: Advances in theory, research and practice*. Herefordshire, England: PCCS Books.

References

Asay, T. P., & Lambert, M. J. (1999). The empirical case for the common factors in therapy. In M. A. Hubble, B. L. Duncan, & S. D. Miller (Eds.), *The heart and soul of change* (pp. 23–55). Washington, DC: American Psychological Association.

Bachelor, A. (1988). How clients perceive therapist empathy: A content analysis of 'received' empathy. *Psychotherapy, 25*(2), 227–240.

Baldwin, M. (1987). Interview with Carl Rogers on the use of self in therapy. In M. Baldwin & V. Satir (Eds.), *The use of self in therapy* (pp. 45–52). New York, NY: Haworth Press.

Barrett-Lennard, G. T. (2007). The relational foundations of person-centered practice. In M. Cooper, M. O'Hara, P. F. Schmid, & G. Wyatt, *The handbook of person-centered psychotherapy and counseling*. New York, NY: Palgrave McMillan.

Bergin, A. E., & Garfield, S. L. (Eds.). (1994). *Handbook of psychotherapy and behavior change* (4th ed.). New York, NY: Wiley.

Beutler, L. (1999, June). The differential role of therapist relationship skills and techniques in effective psychotherapy. Paper presented at the *Society for Psychotherapy Research*, Braga, Portugal.

Beutler, L. E., & Clarkin, J. F. (1990). *Systematic treatment selection*. New York, NY: Bruner Mazel.

Bohart, A. C. (1998). Review of the book *Successful psychotherapy: A caring, loving relationship. Person-Centered Journal, 5*, 66–70.

Bohart, A. C. (2007). The actualizing person. In M. Cooper, M. O'Hara, P. F. Schmid, & G. Wyatt (Eds.), *The handbook of person-centered psychotherapy and counseling* (pp. 47–63). New York, NY: Palgrave Macmillan.

Bohart, A. C., & Greenberg, L. S. (1997). *Empathy reconsidered: New directions in psychotherapy*. Washington, DC: American Psychological Association.

Bohart, A., & Tallman, K. (1999). *How clients make therapy work: The process of active self-healing*. Washington, DC: American Psychological Association.

Boss, M. (1963). *Psychoanalysis and daisensanalysis*. New York, NY: Basic Books.

Bozarth, J. D. (2002). The nondirective attitude in client-centered therapy. *Journal of Humanistic Psychology, 42*(2), 78–83.

Bozarth, J. D., Zimring, F. M., & Tausch, R. (2002). Client-centered therapy: The evolution of a revolution. In D. J. Cain & J. Seeman (Eds.), *Humanistic psychotherapies: Handbook of research and practice* (pp. 147–188). Washington, DC: American Psychological Association.

Brodley, B. T., & Brody, A. F. (1990, August). Understanding client-centered therapy through interviews conducted by Carl Rogers. Paper presented at the annual convention of the American Psychological Association, Boston.

Buber, M. (1958). *I and thou* (R. G. Smith, Trans., 2nd rev. ed.). New York, NY: Scribner.

Burckell, L. A., & Goldfried, M. R. (2006).Therapist qualities preferred by sexual-minority individuals. *Psychotherapy: Theory, Research, Practice, Training, 43*(1), 32–49.

Burton, A. (1972). *Twelve therapists.* San Francisco, CA: Jossey-Bass.

Cain, D. J. (1989). The paradox of nondirectiveness in the person-centered approach. *Person-Centered Review, 4*(2), 123–131.

Cain, D. J. (1990). Further thoughts about nondirectiveness and client-centered therapy. *Person-Centered Review, 5*(1), 89–99.

Cain, D. J. (1996). Rogers and Sylvia: An intimate and affirming encounter. In B. A. Farber, D. C. Brink, & P. M. Raskin (Eds.), *The psychotherapy of Carl Rogers* (pp. 275–283). New York, NY: Guilford Press.

Clarkin, J. F., & Levy, K. N. (2004). The influence of client variables on psychotherapy. In M. J. Lambert (Ed.), *Bergin and Garfield's handbook of psychotherapy and behavior change* (5th ed., pp. 194–226). New York, NY: Wiley.

Combs, A. W. (1986). What makes a good helper? *Person-Centered Review, 1*(1), 51–61.

Combs, A. W. (1989). *A theory of therapy.* Newbury Park, CA: Sage.

Combs, A. W. (1999). *Being and becoming.* New York, NY: Springer.

Conte, H. R., Ratto, R., Clutz, K., & Karasu, T. B. (1995). Determinants of outpatients' satisfaction with therapists—relation to outcome. *Journal of Psychotherapy Practice and Research, 4*(1), 43–51.

Cooper, M. (2003). Between freedom and despair: Existential challenges and contributions to person-centered and experiential therapy. *Person-Centered and Experiential Psychotherapies, 2*(1), 43–56.

Cooper, M. (2004). Existential approaches to psychotherapy. In P. Sanders (Ed.), *The tribes of the person-centered nation* (pp. 95–124). Ross-on-Wye, England: PCCS Books.

Cooper, M. (2008). *Essential research findings in counseling and psychotherapy.* London, England: Sage.

Cooper, M., O'Hara, M., Schmid, P. F., & Wyatt, G. (2007). *The handbook of person-centered psychotherapy and counseling.* New York, NY: Palgrave Macmillan.

Cornelius-White, J., & Cornelius-White, C. (2005). Reminiscing and predicting: Rogers's beyond words speech and commentary. *Journal of Humanistic Psychology, 45*(3), 383–396.

Corsini, R. J., & Auerbach, A. J. (Eds.). (1998). *Concise encyclopedia of psychology.* New York, NY: Wiley.

Damasio, A. R. (1994). *Decartes' error.* New York, NY: Grosset/Putnam.

Dekeyser, M., Prouty, G., & Elliott, R. (2008). Pre-therapy process and outcome: A review of research instruments and findings. *Person-Centered and Experiential Psychotherapies, 7*(1), 37–55.

Elliott, R. (1985). Helpful and nonhelpful events in in brief counseling interviews: An empirical taxonomy. *Journal of Counseling Psychology, 32,* 307–322.

Elliott, R., & Greenberg, L.S. (2002). Process-experiential psychotherapy. In D. J. Cain & J. Seeman (Eds.), *Humanistic psychotherapies: Handbook of research and practice.* (pp. 279–306). Washington, DC: American Psychological Association.

Elliott, R., Greenberg, L. S., & Lietaer, G. (2004). Research on experiential psychotherapies. In M. J. Lambert (Ed.), *Bergin and Garfield's handbook of psychotherapy and behavior change* (5th ed., pp. 493–539). New York, NY: Wiley.

Elliott, R., Watson, J. C., Goldman, R. N., & Greenberg, L. S. (2004). *Learning emotion focused therapy.* Washington, DC: American Psychological Association.

Farber, B. A., Brink, D. C., & Raskin, P. M. (Eds.). (1996). *The psychotherapy of Carl Rogers: Cases and commentary.* New York, NY: Guilford Press.

Farber, B. A., & Lane, J. S. (2002). Positive regard. In J. C. Norcross (Ed.), *Psychotherapy relationships that work* (pp. 175–194). New York, NY: Oxford University Press.

Feifel, H., & Eels, J. (1963). Patients and therapists assess the same therapy. *Journal of Consulting Psychology, 27*(4), 310–318.

Foa, E. B., & Jaycox, L. H. (1999). Cognitive-behavioral treatment of posttraumatic stress disorder. In D. Spiegel (Ed.), *Efficacy and cost-effectiveness of psychotherapy* (pp. 23–61). Washington, DC: American Psychiatric Publishing.

Francis, K. C. (2009). Questions and answers: Two hours with Carl Rogers. *Person-Centered Journal, 16* (1–2), 4–35.

Frankl, V. E. (1963). *Man's search for meaning.* New York, NY: Washington Square Press.

Frankl, V. E. (1967). *Psychotherapy and existentialism.* New York, NY: Clarion.

Friedman, M. (1985). *The healing dialogue in psychotherapy.* New York, NY: Jason Aronson.

Friedman, M. (1986). Carl Rogers and Martin Buber. *Person-Centered Review, 1*(4), 409–435.

Friedman, M. (1992). *Dialogue and the human image.* Newbury Park, CA: Sage.

Friedman, M. (2002). Martin Buber and dialogical psychotherapy. *Journal of Humanistic Psychology, 42*(4), 7–36.

Gendlin, E. T. (1970). A theory of personality change. In J. T Hart & T. M. Tomlinson (Eds.), *New directions in client-centered psychotherapy* (pp. 129–173). Boston, MA: Houghton Mifflin.

Gendlin, E. T. (1986). Talk on Experiential Focusing and Rogers's Contributions [Videotape]. Presented at Beyond Words Symposium at the Chicago Counseling and Psychotherapy Center.

Gendlin, E. T. (1996). *Focusing-oriented psychotherapy.* New York, NY: Guilford Press.

Glass, C. R., & Arnkoff, D. B. (2000). Consumers' perspectives on helpful and hindering factors in mental health treatment. *Journal of Clinical Psychology, 56*(110), 1467–1480.

Goldman, R., Greenberg, L., & Pos, A. (2005). Depth of emotional experience and outcome. *Psychotherapy Research, 15,* 248–260.

Goldman, R. N., Greenberg, L. S., & Angus, L. A. (2006). The effects of adding emotion-focused interventions to the client-centered relationship conditions in the treatment of depression. *Psychotherapy Research, 16*(5), 537–549.

Gordon, T. (1970). *Parent effectiveness training.* New York, NY: Peter H. Wyden.

Grant, B. (2004). The imperative of ethical justification in psychotherapy: The special case of client-centered therapy. *Person-Centered and Experiential Psychotherapies, 3*(3), 152–165.

Greenberg, L. S., Auszra, L., & Herman, I. R. (2007). The relationship among emotional productivity, emotional arousal and outcome in experiential therapy of depression. *Psychotherapy Research, 17*(4), 482–493.

Greenberg, L. S., Elliott, R., & Lietaer, G. (1994). Research on humanistic and experiential psychotherapies. In A. E. Bergin & S. L. Garfield (Eds.), *Handbook of psychotherapy and behavior change* (4th ed., pp. 509–539). New York, NY: Wiley.

Greenberg, L. S., Elliott, R., Watson, J. C., & Bohart, A. C. (2001). Empathy. *Psychotherapy: Theory, Research, Practice, Training, 38*(4), 380–384.

Greenberg, L. S., & Foerster, F. (1996). Resolving unfinished business: The process of change. *Journal of Counseling and Clinical Psychology, 64,* 439–446.

Greenberg, L. S., Korman, L. M., & Pavio, S. C. (2002). Emotion in humanistic psychotherapy. In D. J. Cain & J. Seeman (Eds.), *Humanistic psychotherapies: Handbook of research and practice* (pp. 499–530). Washington, DC: American Psychological Association.

Greenberg, L. S., & Van Balen, R. (1999). The theory of experience-centered therapies. In L. S. Greenberg, J. C. Watson, & G. Lietaer (Eds.), *Handbook of experiential psychotherapy* (pp. 28–57). New York, NY: Guilford Press.

Greenberg, L. S., & Watson, J. C. (2006). *Emotion-focused therapy for depression.* Washington, DC: American Psychological Association.

Grote, B. (2005). The experience of feeling really understood in psychotherapy: A phenomenological study. Unpublished doctoral dissertation.

Hart, J. T., & Tomlinson, T. M. (1970). *New directions in client-centered therapy.* New York, NY: Wiley.

Hendricks, M. N. (2002). Focusing oriented/experiential psychotherapy. In D. J. Cain & J. Seeman (Eds.), *Humanistic psychotherapies: Handbook of research and practice* (pp. 221–251). Washington, DC: American Psychological Association.

Hill, C. E. (2007). My personal reactions to Rogers (1957): The facilitative but neither necessary nor sufficient conditions of therapeutic personality change. *Psychotherapy: Theory, Research, Practice, Training, 44*(3), 260–264.

Hirscheimer, K. (1996). *Development and verification of a measure of unfinished business.* Master's thesis, Department of Psychology, York University, Toronto, Ontario, Canada.

Hobbs, N. (1951). Group-centered psychotherapy. In C. R. Rogers, *Client-centered psychotherapy* (p. 292). Boston, MA: Houghton Mifflin.

Hubble, M. A., Duncan, B. L., & Miller, S. D. (1999). Directing attention to what works. In M. A. Hubble, B. L. Duncan, & S. D. Miller (Eds.), *The heart and soul of change* (pp. 407–447). Washington, DC: American Psychological Association.

Iberg, J. R. (1996). Using statistical experiments with post-session client questionnaires as a student-centered approach to teaching the effects of therapist activities in psychotherapy. In A. Hutterer, R. Pawlowsky, P. F. Schmid & R. Stipsits (Eds.), *Client-centered and experiential psychotherapy: A paradigm in motion* (pp. 255–271). Frankfurt am Main, Germany: Peter Lang.

Johnson, S. M. (2007). The contribution of emotionally focused couples therapy. *Journal of Contemporary Psychotherapy, 37*(1), 47–52.

Johnson, S. M., Hunsley, J., Greenberg, L., & Schindler, D. (1999). Emotionally focused couples therapy: Status & challenges. *Clinical Psychology: Science & Practice, 6,* 67–79.

Jordan, J. V. (1991).The development of women's sense of self. In J. V. Jordan, A. G. Kaplan, J. B. Miller, L. P. Stiver, & J. L. Surrey (Eds.), *Women's growth in connection: Writings from the Stone Center* (pp. 81–96). New York, NY: Guilford Press.

Kirschenbaum, H. (1979). *On becoming Carl Rogers.* New York, NY: Delacorte.

Kirschenbaum, H. (2007). *The life and work of Carl Rogers.* Ross-on-Wye, England: PCCS Books.

Kirschenbaum, H., & Jourdan, A. (2005). The current status of Carl Rogers and the person-centered approach. *Psychotherapy, 42*(1), 37–51.

Klein, M. H., Kolden, G. G., Michels, J. L., & Chisholm-Stockard, S. (2002). Congruence or genuineness. In J. C. Norcross (Ed.), Empirically supported psychotherapy relationships. *Psychotherapy: Theory, Research, Practice, Training, 38*(4), 396–405.

Kluckhohn, C., Murray, H., & Alexander, H. (Eds.). (1959). Personality formation: The determinants. In C. Kluckholm, H. A. Murray, & D. M. Schneider (Eds.), *Personality and nature, society and culture* (pp. 53–67). New York, NY: Knopf.

Koch, S. (Ed.). (1959). *Psychology: A study of a science.* New York, NY: McGraw-Hill.

Laing, R. D. (1969). *The divided self.* Middlesex, England: Penguin.

Lambert, M. J. (1992). Implications of outcome research for psychotherapy integration. In J. C. Norcross & M. R. Goldstein (Eds.), *Handbook of psychotherapy integration.* New York, NY: Basic Books.

Lambert, M. J. (2003). Psychotherapy outcome research: Implications for integrative and eclectic therapists. In J. C. Norcross & M. R. Goldfried (Eds.), *Handbook of psychotherapy integration* (pp. 94–129). New York, NY: Basic Books.

Lazarus, A. A. (2007). On necessity and sufficiency in counseling and psychotherapy (revisited). *Psychotherapy: Theory, Research, Practice, Training, 44*(3), 253–256.

Leijssen, M. (1996). Characteristics of a healing inner relationship. In A. Hutterer, R. Pawlowsky, P. F. Schmid, & R. Stipsits (Eds.), *Client-centered and experiential psychotherapy: A paradigm in motion* (pp. 427–438). Frankfurt am Main, Germany: Peter Lang.

Levant, R., & Shlien, J. (Eds.). (1984). *Client-centered therapy and the person-centered approach.* New York, NY: Praeger.

Lietaer, G. (2001). Unconditional acceptance and positive regard. In J. Bozarth & P. Wilkins (Eds.), *UPR: Unconditional positive regard* (pp. 88–108). Ross-on-Wye, England: PCCS Books.

Lietaer, G., Rombauts, J., & Van Balen, R. (Eds.). (1990). *Client-centered and experiential psychotherapy in the nineties.* Leuven, Belgium: Leuven University Press.

Lindauer, M. S. (1998). The phenomenal method. In R. J. Corsini & A. J. Auerbach (Eds.), *Concise encyclopedia of psychology.* New York, NY: Wiley.

Mac Dougall, C. (2002). Rogers' person-centered approach: Considerations for use in multicultural counseling. *Journal of Humanistic Psychology, 42*(2), 48–65.

Mahoney, M. J. (1991). *Human change processes.* New York, NY: Basic Books.

Mahrer, A. R., Nadler, W. P., Dessaulles, A., Gervaize, P. A., & Sterner, I. (1987). Good and very good moments in psychotherapy: Content, distribution, and facilitation. *Psychotherapy, 24,* 7–14.

Mahrer, A. (2007). To a large extent, the field got it wrong: New learnings from a new look at an old classic. *Psychotherapy: Theory, Research, Practice, Training, 44*(3), 274–278.

Malcolm, W. (1999). *Relating process to outcome in the treatment of unfinished business in process experiential therapy.* Unpublished doctoral dissertation, York University, Toronto, Ontario, Canada.

Maslow, A. H. (1987). *Motivation and personality.* New York, NY: Harper and Row.

May, R. (1958). *Existence: A new dimension in psychiatry and psychology.* New York, NY: Simon and Schuster.

Mearns, D., & Cooper, M. (2005). *Working at relational depth in counseling and psychotherapy.* London, England: Sage.

Mearns, D., & Thorne, B. (2007). *Person-centered counseling in action* (3rd ed.). London, England: Sage.

Merrill, C., & Anderson, S. (1993). A content analysis of person-centered expressive therapy outcomes. *The Humanistic Psychologist, 21,* 354–363.

Miller, S. D., Duncan, B. L., & Hubble, M. A. (1997). *Escape from Babel.* New York, NY: Norton.

Missirlian, T., Toukmanian, S., Warwar, S., &. Greenberg, L. (2005). Emotional arousal, client perceptual processing, and the working alliance in experiential psychotherapy for depression. *Journal of Consulting & Clinical Psychology, 73*(5), 861–871.

Mohr, D. C. (1995).Negative outcome in psychotherapy—a critical review. *Clinical Psychology: Science and Practice, 2*(1), 1–27.

Moustakas, C. E. (1995). *Being-in, being-for, being-with.* Northvale, NJ: Jason Aronson.

Nicholas, M. (1994). *The mystery of goodness and the positive moral consequences of psychotherapy.* New York, NY: Norton.

Orlinsky, D. E., Grawe, K., & Parks, B. K. (1994). Process and outcome in psychotherapy: *Noch einmal.* In S. L. Garfield & A. E. Bergin (Eds.), *Handbook of psychotherapy and behavior change* (4th ed., pp. 270–376). New York, NY: Wiley.

Ornish, D. (1997). *Love and survival.* New York, NY: Harper Collins.

Paivio, S., & Greenberg, L. (1995). Resolving unfinished business: Efficacy of experiential therapy using empty-chair dialogue. *Journal of Consulting and Clinical Psychology, 63,* 419–425.

Patterson, C. H. (1996). Multicultural counseling: From diversity to universality. *Journal of Counseling and Development, 74,* 227–231.

Paulson, B. L., Everall, R. D., & Janice, S. (2002). Client perception of hindering experiences in counseling. *Counseling and Psychotherapy Research, 1*(1), 53–61.

Pedersen, P. B. (1991). Multiculturalism as a generic approach to counseling. *Journal of Counseling & Development, 70,* 6–12.

Pedersen, P. B., Lonner, W., & Draguns, J. (Eds.). (1976). *Counseling across cultures.* Honolulu, HI: University Press of Hawaii.

Prouty, G. (1994). *Theoretical evolutions in person-centered/experiential therapy applications to schizophrenic and retarded psychoses.* Westport, CT: Praeger.

Prouty, G. (1999). Pre-therapy and pre-symbolic experiencing evolutions in person-centered/experiential approaches. In L. S. Greenberg, J. C. Watson & G. Lietaer (Eds.), *Handbook of experiential psychotherapy* (pp. 388–409). New York, NY: Guilford Press.

Prouty, G., VanWerde, D., & Portner, M. (2002). *Pre-therapy: Reaching contact-impaired clients.* Ross-on-Wye, England: PCCS Books.

Rennie, D. L. (2002). Experiencing psychotherapy: Grounded theory studies. In D. J. Cain & J. Seeman (Eds.), *Humanistic psychotherapies: Handbook of research and practice* (pp. 117–144). Washington, DC: American Psychological Association.

Rice, L. N. (1974). The evocative function of the therapist. In D. A. Wexler & L. N. Rice (Eds.), *Innovations in client-centered therapy* (pp. 289–311). New York, NY: Wiley.

Rogers, C. R. (1937). *Clinical treatment of the problem child.* Boston, MA: Houghton Mifflin.

Rogers, C. R. (1942). *Counseling and psychotherapy.* Boston, MA: Houghton Mifflin.

Rogers, C. R. (1951). *Client-centered Therapy.* Boston, MA: Houghton Mifflin.

Rogers, C. R. (1957). The necessary and sufficient conditions of therapeutic personality change. *Journal of Consulting Psychology, 21*(2), 95–103.

Rogers, C. R. (1959). A theory of therapy, personality, and interpersonal relationships as developed in the client-centered framework. In S. Koch (Ed.), *Psychology: A study of science, Vol. 3 Formulations of the person and the social context* (pp. 184–256). New York, NY: McGraw-Hill.

Rogers, C. R. (1961). *On becoming a person.* Boston, MA: Houghton Mifflin.

Rogers, C. R. (1967). *The therapeutic relationship and its impact: A study of psychotherapy with schizophrenics.* Madison: University of Wisconsin Press.

Rogers, C. R. (1970). *Carl Rogers on encounter groups.* New York, NY: Harper & Row.

Rogers, C. R. (1972). My personal growth. In A. Burton (Ed.), *Twelve therapists* (pp. 28–77). San Francisco, CA: Jossey-Bass.

Rogers, C. R. (1977). *Carl Rogers on personal power.* New York, NY: Delacorte.

Rogers, C. R. (1980). *A way of being.* Boston, MA: Houghton Mifflin.

Rogers, C. R. (1986). A comment from Carl Rogers. *Person-Centered Review, 1,* 3–5.

Rogers, C., & Dymond, R. (1954). *Psychotherapy and personality change.* Chicago, IL: University of Chicago Press.

Rogers, C. R., & Sanford, R. C. (1989). Client-centered psychotherapy. In H. I. Kaplan & B. J. Sadock (Eds), *Comprehensive handbook of psychiatry* (pp. 1482–1501). Baltimore, MD: Williams & Wilkins.

Rogers, C. R., & Stevens, B. (1967). *Person to person: The problem of being human.* New York, NY: Pocket Books.

Rogers, C. R., Perls, F. S., & Ellis, A. (1965). *Three approaches to psychotherapy* [Film]. Psychological Films, Inc.

Rogers, N. (n.d.). Welcome to my website. Retrieved October 2, 2009, from http://www.nrogers.com.

Sachse, R., & Elliott, R. (2002). Process-outcome research on humanistic therapy variables. In D. J. Cain & J. Seeman (Eds.), *Humanistic psychotherapies: Handbook of research and practice* (pp. 83–115). Washington, DC: American Psychological Association.

Safran, J. D., Muran, J. C., & Samstag, L. W. (1994). Resolving therapeutic alliance ruptures: A task analytic investigation. In A. O. Horvath & L. S. Greenberg (Eds.), *The working alliance: Theory, research, and practice* (pp. 225–255). New York, NY: Wiley.

Samstag, L. W. (2007). The necessary and sufficient conditions of therapeutic personality change: Reaction to Rogers's 1957 article. *Psychotherapy: Theory, Research, Practice, Training, 44*(3), 295–299.

Sanders, P. (Ed.). (2004). *The tribes of the person-centered nation.* Ross-on-Wye, England: PCCS Books.

Schneider, K. J., & May, R. (1995). *The psychology of existence.* New York, NY: McGraw-Hill.

Seeman, J. (1965). Perspectives in client-centered therapy. In B. B.Wolman (Ed.), *Handbook of clinical psychology* (pp. 1215–1229). New York, NY: McGraw-Hill.

Seeman, J. (1988). Self-actualization: A reformulation. *Person-Centered Review, 3*(2), 304–315.

Seeman, J. (2002). Looking back, looking ahead: A synthesis. In D. J. Cain & J. Seeman (Eds.), *Humanistic psychotherapies: Handbook of research and practice* (pp. 617–636). Washington, DC: American Psychological Association.

Shlien, J. M. (2003). *To lead an honorable life.* Ross-on-Wye, England: PCCS Books.

Silberschatz, G. (2007). Comments on "the necessary and sufficient conditions of therapeutic personality change." *Psychotherapy: Theory, Research, Practice, Training, 44*(3), 265–267.

Smith, D. (1982). Trends in counseling and psychotherapy. *American Psychologist, 37*, 802–809.

Sue, D. W., & Sue, D. (1990). *Counseling the culturally different: Theory and practice* (2nd ed.). New York, NY: Wiley.

Sue, S. (1983). Ethnic minorities in psychology: A reexamination. *American Psychologist, 38*, 583–592.

Sullivan, H. S. (1947). *Conceptions of modern psychiatry.* Washington, DC: William Alanson White Foundation.

Taft, J. (1933). *The dynamics of therapy in a controlled relationship.* New York, NY: Macmillan.

Tageson, C. W. (1982). *Humanistic psychology: A synthesis.* Homewood, IL: Dorsey Press.

The top 10: The most influential therapists of the past quarter-century. (2007, April). *The Psychotherapy Networker.*

Truax, C. B., & Carkhuff, R. R. (1967). *Toward effective counseling and psychotherapy.* Chicago, IL: Aldine.

Truax, C. B., & Mitchell, K. M. (1971). Research on certain therapist interpersonal skills in relation to process and outcome. In A. E. Bergin & S. L. Garfield

(Eds.), *Handbook of psychotherapy and behavior change* (pp. 299–344). New York, NY: Wiley.

Twenge, J. M. (2006). *Generation me.* New York, NY: Free Press.

Vollmer, B., Grote, J., Lange, R., & Walker, C. (2009). A therapy preferences interview: Empowering clients by offering choices. *Psychotherapy Bulletin, 44*(2), 33–37.

Wachtel, P. L. (2007). Carl Rogers and the larger context of therapeutic thought. *Psychotherapy: Theory, Research, Practice, Training, 44,* 279–284.

Warner, M. (2000). Person-centered psychotherapy: One nation, many tribes. *Person-Centered Journal, 7*(1), 28–39.

Warwar, N., & Greenberg, L. (1999, June). Emotional processing and therapeutic change. Paper presented at the International Society for Psychotherapy Research Annual Meeting, Braga, Portugal.

Watson, J. C. (2002). Re-visioning empathy: Research, practice and theory. In D. J. Cain & J. Seeman (Eds.), *Humanistic psychotherapies: Handbook of research and practice* (pp. 445–471). Washington, DC: American Psychological Association.

Watson, J. C., Goldman, R. N., & Warner, M. S. (Eds.). (2002). *Client-centered and experiential psychotherapy: Advances in theory, research and practice.* Ross-on-Wye, England: PCCS Books.

Watson, J. C., Greenberg, L. S., & Lietaer, G. (1998). The experiential paradigm unfolding. In L. S. Greenberg, J. C. Watson, & G. Lietaer (Eds.), *Handbook of experiential psychotherapy* (pp. 1–27). New York, NY: Guilford Press.

Watson, N. (1984). The empirical status of Rogers's hypothesis of the necessary and sufficient conditions for effective psychotherapy. In R. E. Levant & J. M. Shlien (Eds.), *Client-centered therapy and the person-centered approach* (pp. 17–40). New York, NY: Praeger.

Wexler, D., & Rice, L. (1974). *Innovations in client-centered therapy.* New York, NY: Wiley.

Wolman, B. B. (Ed.). (1965). *Handbook of clinical psychology.* New York, NY: McGraw-Hill.

Worsley, R. (2004). Integrating with integrity. In P. Sanders (Ed.), *The tribes of the person-centered nation* (pp. 125–147). Ross-on-Wye, England: PCCS Books.

Yalom, I. (1980). *Existential psychotherapy.* New York, NY: Basic Books.

Yalom, I. (1989). *Love's executioner.* New York, NY: Basic Books.

Yontef, G. (1993). *Awareness, dialogue and process: Essay in gestalt therapy.* Highland, NY: Gestalt Journal Press.

Yontef, G. (2007). The power of the immediate moment in gestalt therapy. *Journal of Contemporary Psychotherapy, 37*(1), 17–23.

Zimring, F. M., & Raskin, N. J. (1992). Carl Rogers and client/person-centered therapy. In D. K, Freedhelm (Ed.), *History of psychotherapy* (pp. 629–656). Washington, DC: American Psychological Association.

Index

About the Author

David J. Cain, PhD, ABPP, is the editor of *Humanistic Psychotherapies: Handbook of Research and Practice* (2002) and of *Classics in the Person-Centered Approach* (2002). He received his doctorate in clinical and community psychology from the University of Wyoming. At present, he teaches at the California School of Professional Psychology at Alliant International University, San Diego, and in the psychology department at Chapman University. A former colleague of Carl Rogers, he is the founder of the Association for the Development of the Person-Centered Approach and was the founder and editor of the *Person-Centered Review*. He is a diplomate and fellow in clinical psychology of the American Board of Professional Psychology and a member of the National Register of Certified Group Psychotherapists. Dr. Cain is the psychotherapy editor for the *Journal of Humanistic Psychology* and serves on the editorial boards of *The Humanistic Psychologist, Person-Centered and Experiential Psychotherapies, Person-Centered Journal,* and the *Journal of Contemporary Psychotherapy.* He edited a special issue of the *Journal of Humanistic Psychotherapy* entitled "Advancing Humanistic Psychology in the 21st Century" and edited a special issue of the *Journal of Contemporary Psychotherapy* entitled "Contributions of Humanistic Psychotherapies to the Field of Psychotherapy." Dr. Cain is a former president of the Society for Humanistic Psychology of the American Psychological Association and initiated its first annual conference. His primary professional commitment is the advancement of humanistic psychology and psychotherapy. He maintains a private practice in Carlsbad and San Marcos, California.